The Art Course

Tom Robb

The Art Course

From 30-minute sketches to week-long paintings –
60 complete drawing and painting projects
timed to develop your technique

Tom Robb

CRESCENT BOOKS
NEW YORK

This 1990 edition published by CRESCENT BOOKS,
distributed by Outlet Book Company, Inc.,
a Random House Company, 225 Park Avenue South,
New York, New York 10003.

Typeset by Tradespools, Frome

Originated by Columbia Offset, Singapore

Printed in Hong Kong

ISBN 0-517-053802

8   7   6   5   4   3   2   1

With many thanks to all my friends
who have worked with me over the
years, and who by their knowledge,
enthusiasm, and continual encouragement
to student and fellow teacher alike
have contributed so much
to the enjoyment of life

Tom Robb 1988

Contents

Introducing the art school

Learning to be an artist started with human society as a family affair; after a period of local independence, when everyone was involved only in their own needs, the era of specialization began. First the tribes with access to local raw materials became more adept at their use, and so created a market in pottery, glassware, bronzes or wood carvings.

Then gradually, one family would make all the baskets, another the pots, yet another the totems or carvings. Skills and techniques were passed as a great treasure from parent to child, to be passed on in turn to even younger children as they grew to the age of initiation. Of course within the family there were degrees of excellence, and a few, a very few individual names have been recorded – but talent was a resource for the community, to be used for the good of the tribe and for the benefit of all.

Even as late as the medieval period, a kind of tribal family was still in existence, in the institutions known as craft guilds. However, the population explosion after the plague years caused such a demand that talent had to found outside, and brought into the guild, through hard and long apprenticeship. The major patron remained the community, although embodied in the church and the castle rather than the tribe.

In fact, although it is common practice to speak of the church as the greatest patron of art until the Renaissance, the aristocratic medieval home in England, France and Italy was decorated and embellished with tapestries to keep out the cold winds, clothes were embroidered with fur and jewels for both status and warmth, portable altars bejewelled as well, and painted in the most expensive pigments of lapis lazuli and gold, delectable illuminated books were carefully put together for the lords and ladies to hold in the hand, and brilliantly ornamented domestic utensils for personal care, for hair powders, face colours and perfume were made for gifts and offerings.

Indeed, whatever delights they had known before, once the Crusades had introduced the soldiers of Christ to the glorious arts of the Middle East, life in the northern castles would never be the same. The Renaissance Man, that figment of our imagination who painted a little, who sang and wrote music, who tossed off a poem before breakfast and the design for a palazzo after lunch, had actually been around long before the era of the Medicis, in the courtiers of the king's household, in the troubadours who were also the confidants of queens, and the poets like Chaucer who were

also remarkably able diplomats and civil servants in an increasingly demanding state beaurocracy.

Yet even as the multi-talented amateur enjoyed every opportunity to explore the world, the time of the professional artist had begun; an individual, revered and respected not only for technical excellence, or for skill in manufacture, but for the gift of interpretation, for a feeling of exaltation in carrying out a theme, and who was often credited with almost divine inspiration.

With the great masters of the Renaissance, and the demands of state patronage for grand works of art to be displayed in palaces and civic buildings, formal art training developed, centred around individual artists who, for the first time, were not part of the church or monastery.

Apprentices were required to help cope with the mounting flood of commissions, and the masters welcomed a contribution of money from parents anxious to see their sons established later in life. These assistants, who were usually accepted only after they had shown they could draw, worked in a way that art school students today would find unbelieveable – there was seldom a rest from the labour of grinding pigments, hauling stone and roughing out fresco paintings or carved frames. Some students were kept on for the sheer effort of their eyes and arms, some for the talent which could be put to use in making preliminary drawings, background draperies, and details of the large expanses of wall and canvas which the artist was expected to produce for his patron's home or public building.

In turn, the young assistants learned what they could, and went out to find patrons of their own.

But soon the apprenticeship family was eroded by the changes in society. With the drop in church and state patronage, and the rapid growth of new private patrons demanding smaller paintings and sculptures for their homes, the most popular artists had little need for swarms of very young students. By the 1700s, pupils grew older and fewer in number, patrons demanded, as their modern counterparts often do, only the well-known reputations, and many young would-be artists found themselves unable to find any kind of training. If they were talented in catching a likeness, then portraits were always in demand, and a journeyman painter could travel the length and breadth of the land, painting inn signs, landlord's daughters and local yeoman families, teaching a little drawing to the ladies, and making a respectable living. Otherwise, life was increasingly difficult for anyone wanting to study with established teachers.

However, by the eighteenth century there were fine painting academies abroad, particularly in Italy, visited by young noblemen on the Grand Tour who paid to go a life class or two, or attend a discussion on landscape drawing. The idea of an academy in England as a professional training base grew, and in the mid-1700s the Royal Academy was established in London to provide artist-teachers for the best of the young students. The rise, too, of professional colourmen and art material suppliers meant that much of the previous work done by underpaid, underage apprentices was now unnecessary, and the students could concentrate on a systematic course of art history and practical study of the past, as well as classes in the development of skills. Art academies also gave entry into public exhibitions, led to professional qualifications and the possibility of finding buyers and employment.

Once the academy was established, even newer ideas began to thrive; the more rebellious young students scorned the idea of studying the old masters, and devoted themselves to going out into the landscape and looking for themselves, learning to record what they saw as Turner, Constable and Cezanne had done. Studying indoors and copying other people's ideas were considered stultifying and uninspired, fit only for those who could teach but not paint themselves. The artist had left the tribal family behind again, becoming more and more inbued with the idea of the individual worth, the individual statement, the unique power of a particular artistic impression.

Today we are in the midst of another great change. After the shock of the twentieth century "ism" and the growth of abstract art which seemed to owe nothing to traditional training, the art world has turned again to recognize the skills of being able to look and record with accuracy and intelligence. Art school training is in such demand that for every successful applicant there are at least four or five who will not be able to find a place. And more and more people, thwarted of the chance to study art at school, are finding art instruction books and courses a lifeline to rich personal experience. None is denied a chance, everyone can participate in the heritage which 5000 years of the practice of art has left us.

The leisure artists

Just as the art school student has changed radically in the past so the leisure artist has taken on a very different role in the painter's world.

Calling someone an 'amateur' was once a word of praise and commendation – a lover of the arts, made of finer stuff than the humdrum professional, capable of the greatest inspiration and feeling, even when practical skills were lacking. With rare exceptions, only someone with enough money to afford the time to paint purely for the pleasure of it was an amateur, and by that very requirement likely to be a gentleman or lady.

Then the amateur was considered a tiresome interruption in the life of a professional, too much a diletante to do any serious work, and too imbued with nonsensical ideals to make a real contribution to art.

Happily that too has passed. Today the leisure painter is the centre of a new industry, and art has returned to its proper place as a source of great pleasure and delight for anyone who cares to take a little time in discovering its many treasures. A little time is all that is necessary to begin, and that is what this book is about – time to paint, for everyone.

Introduction to drawing

Anyone can learn to draw; a simple statement that sounds almost impossible, but nonetheless is true, because drawing has its roots in the fundamentals of making marks, and we all make marks from the time we begin to hold a piece of chalk or crayon.

What is a reasonable definition of drawing? Almost every statement has to have its qualifier; if we say that drawing is based on describing outline, we have to take into account the incredible tone drawings of artists like Turner and Monet. If we say that it is based on black and white, there are the sepia and brick-red drawings of the great masters, and all the multiplicity and multi-colourings of drawings in crayons and pastels.

And if we try to say that drawings are on paper, as indeed most of them are, we have to remember the many drawings on canvas or wood, using oils or tempera.

So perhaps it makes sense to agree that there is no easy way to separate drawing from painting, but for the purposes of this study we will accept that drawing is the tool of any artist which establishes line, shape and form on any surface, without depending on the use of colour.

Drawing has a very long history, beginning with the first scratched images found on the rocks where men and women lived thousands of centuries ago. These prehistoric works are a revelation – full of life and spirit, often amazingly accurate, and drawn with expertise and skill in charcoal, or a kind of clay paste.

There were decorative borders drawn on pots and utensils as well as walls; the Egyptians had already developed sharpened reeds to use as drawing tools long before the Romans invented the first bronze pens.

By the medieval period, ink and charcoal were commonly used for drawing on manuscripts, either left as they were or coloured in with water-based paints. Renaissance artists had a long apprenticeship in drawing from models, or from life in the crowded, busy streets; they used mainly charcoal and chalks. Young assistants were set to copying the drawings of their teachers, so that everyone in the studio would be capable of helping to draw in the outlines of commissioned paintings and frescoes.

In the 1700s the graphite pencil was invented, bringing an enormous flexibility to drawing of all kinds. It was clean, precise and easy to use. Pastels, too, were now produced in many colours and textures, so that by the end of the century all the necessary tools for the modern draughtsman had been developed, and it could be said that drawing had finally come of age; instead of being regarded somewhat slightingly as a preliminary tool of the artist to be used only as sketches for other works, or underneath a finished painting, drawings were, and are today, admired and collected for their own qualities.

For the aspiring artist, drawing highlights the ability to see, to observe, and to put down what is seen with clarity and economy. No matter how far a painter strays into the realms of colour, or a sculptor creates in three dimensions, and regardless of whether the work is abstract or realistic, drawing is the skeleton, the bones, the fundamental tool of art.

The materials of drawing

Pencils are sticks of wood enclosing today a combination of graphite and clay. The wood is only a protective case for the very fragile rod, and most of us, even art students, do not realize how fragile a pencil is. Dropping a pencil on a hard floor can shatter the graphite, even if the wood stays intact, and although in normal use that would make little difference, once you start sharpening the rod to give your drawings a fine line the pieces of graphite will start dropping out, leaving you eventually with an unusable stub. Modern pencils come in fifteen degrees of hardness, from 6H, the hardest, to 6B, the softest. HB is the centre of the range, and it is used for writing as well as drawing. Try working with a 4H for precision, and with 6B for a lovely fat, dark line, almost like pure charcoal.

Pens are even more varied, with a range of nibs which cover thick and thinness, as well as special curves and angles to help you in calligraphy and shaded curves. Fine mapping pens are used in precision drawing and botanical studies; modern felt-tip pens are an under-utilized resource, with a broad, sweeping feel which can almost paint the paper with ink.

Cartridge pens are not quite as varied, although they are much more convenient, but do try out the pleasures of using nib pens and ink direct from the bottle.

Inks have also been developed for modern designers with dozens of fairly unsubtle colours, although india ink is still the best drawing medium.

If you are experimenting with ink and wash, use black or grey watercolour for the wash

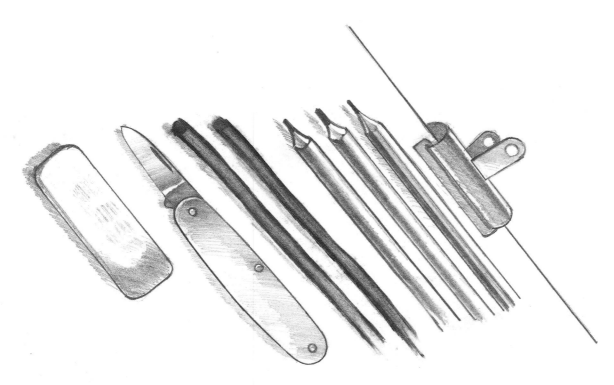

instead of diluted ink – it is better for your brushes.

Cane pens were made by artists for thousands of years, and they still come in handy when you are roaming around out of doors. Make them from sticks of the common bamboo plant or a reed, in lengths of about 8 inches (20cm), and sharpened with a penknife to a sharp or broad nib, as you please.

Chalks come in a variety of basic browns, blacks and whites. Conté sticks, made from a special formula, are easier to use, and also come in wrapped sticks so that your fingers stay a little cleaner.

Charcoal is still a basic drawing tool, made from finely burned wood, split into thick, medium or thin sticks. There are also charcoal pencils which are enclosed in a wooden protective sleeve, but I never feel they have the same expressive texture as the ordinary sticks.

Pastels are the most recent innovation; today there are classic pastels, made with almost all pigment and chalk and just a little gum, and richer oil pastels which give a more intense colour, but with the same flaky texture.

They are not easily blended, and so pastel manufacturers make an incredible number of different colours; unlike oils and watercolours, there seems to be no accepted names for the different shades, so it is really up to you to choose an assortment which covers most of your own requirements. Boxes of mixed pastels usually have a good assortment.

Chalks, charcoal and pastels are all intensely fragile tools; keep them protected in closed boxes when you carry them around. They will also need fixative to keep them on the paper – any good proprietary brand will do. Follow the instructions, and fix all your drawings immediately after you finish them, or you will have nothing left but a few dirty flakes.

Paper is the obvious support for your drawings, and it comes in hundreds of shades and finishes. On the whole, the smoother cartridge papers are best for drawing and sketching, and the ordinary pads are economical. But do try various surface textures shown later in the book; chalks and pastels in particular often benefit from the added colour and texture of the Ingres papers.

Project: learning to use pastels

Above are just some of the ways you can play with different pastel mixes until you discover what kind of textures and tonal qualities you want to use. Try scribbling a range of basic colours on one sheet, and then practice blending them on another part of the paper.

Look at the variations you can get by using the edge of the point, or a small piece of the stick, laid flat and used to make broad strokes.

Test the pressure you need, as well; most beginners use too light a touch, and the painting blows away even before you can get out the fixative. In spite of its name, pastel chalks can give you very bright and assertive colourings if you use them with a firm hand, but never put the pressure on unevenly, or the chalks will break up into fragments.

Keep your scraps of paper to make a sheet of colour codes for yourself, and write on them the colour you used on each section. This is particularly important with pastels – many of the various tones are given brand names, and the mixtures do vary a lot between the different companies. If you enjoy using unusual colour combinations then a pastel scrapbook comes in handy when you need to restock, or while you are working on a drawing.

Drawing Project; the basics of observation, line and tone

The most wonderful thing about drawing is that it is instantly there – a line on the page, and your drawing is started. This project is a way of beginning to draw and beginning to see, as well, which might help you to understand the tools of drawing and observation you are going to need throughout all your time spent in painting.

Imagine that you are looking at a chair. Your brain makes an image, and then starts to check back into memory to see if it can find a similar image. When it does so, a few hints are usually enough for the brain to tell you what you are seeing – a seat and four legs, for example. Your brain now says to itself – Ah, a chair.

This is where the trained artist goes beyond to see rather differently. After the first recognition of a chair, the artist's eye begins to look for selected aspects of that particular chair which are interesting or different. What makes this chair so distinctive? Why this leg, this kind of construction, this shape of back, this turn of foot?

Equipment

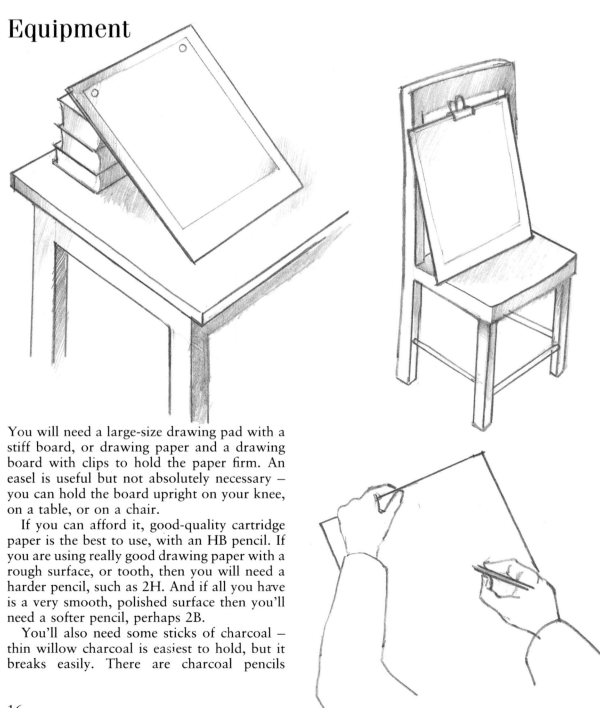

You will need a large-size drawing pad with a stiff board, or drawing paper and a drawing board with clips to hold the paper firm. An easel is useful but not absolutely necessary – you can hold the board upright on your knee, on a table, or on a chair.

If you can afford it, good-quality cartridge paper is the best to use, with an HB pencil. If you are using really good drawing paper with a rough surface, or tooth, then you will need a harder pencil, such as 2H. And if all you have is a very smooth, polished surface then you'll need a softer pencil, perhaps 2B.

You'll also need some sticks of charcoal – thin willow charcoal is easiest to hold, but it breaks easily. There are charcoal pencils which have paper cases that protect your hands a little bit. Wooden-cased charcoal is difficult to sharpen.

Finally, you'll need a sharpener and an eraser.

First step: awareness

Begin with a large piece of paper (at least A3), a pencil and a chair. Place the chair in front of you straight on, so that it is relatively easy to see in outline. Put your own chair 5–6 ft (1.5–2 m) away.

Finding sight size

You will usually be working around arm's length from the paper. When you are a novice draughtsman whatever you are seeing should ideally be sight size; that is, the object when it is drawn on the paper should be around the same size as it appears to be when you look up. You are really making life very difficult for yourself if you have to multiply or reduce sizes in your head all the time. If you have trouble in establishing sight size, hold a piece of transparent paper up in front of you so you can see the chair through it, mark the top and bottom of the chair lightly, then transfer those marks to your sheet of drawing paper. Move yourself (or the chair) backwards or forwards until you have the right size.

An even simpler way is to make a mark about 2 inches (5 cm) from the top of the paper at the edge. Then hold the paper up and move until the image fills the paper comfortably, from your mark down.

Beginning to work

Look from the chair to the paper and from the paper to the chair until you can see the chair on the paper in your mind. Use your brain as a projector, making sure that the image of the chair fills the whole paper.

Fix your parameters by putting a dot where the bottom of each leg is, where the seat is, and so on.

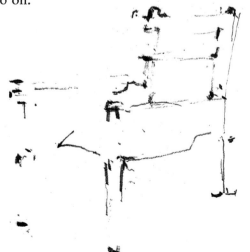

When you are placing these marks, there are questions you need to ask yourself.

Are the legs narrower at the top or bottom? Do they taper a lot, or only a little?

How wide is the leg nearest you in relation to the leg which is furthest away? Half as wide? Twice as wide?

How big is the front edge of the seat in relation to the back edge?

How wide is the seat in relation to the length of the legs? Are they shorter? Taller?

How high is the back in relation to the length of the legs? How wide is the back in relation to its own height?

What is the distance between the two front legs? And between the two back legs?

Now connect the dots, as freely as you can, but nonetheless keeping to the outline. When you have finished you should have a pretty accurate line drawing of the outline of the chair.

Practise doing this with all sorts of objects, drawing them in isolation floating freely on the page, without relating them to their environment in any way. Use whatever you find interesting; still lifes, landscape, people, flowers – anything you want to draw. You'll only master the art of seeing by learning to look, record what you see, and judge the proportions of what you are drawing. If you work well with this kind of discipline you are learning natural perspective as well as you could from any theoretical concept.

Second step: learning about tone

Although the idea of tone can be bewildering to the beginner because we live in a world that is saturated in colour, tone is a word that is used all the time by artists and it is absolutely vital to understand what it means.

Tone is simply the intensity of light and dark. There are two sorts of tone: self-tone, when the colour itself is lighter or darker; and tone caused by light falling on the object, creating highlights and shadows. Although in practice the artist will often be recording them together when he makes a drawing, they are in fact quite distinct, and they make up the form and mass of everything in our world.

Here are two examples of two or three objects which show the two kinds of tone separately and together.

Starting to make tone drawings

Begin as you did before, with the object sight size in front of you, a large piece of good-quality paper, and a stick of thin willow charcoal. Hold the charcoal just like a pencil, in a relaxed but firm fashion. The easel or drawing board should be vertical and at arm's length.

Look at the tone of the object itself: which parts are light and which are dark?

Here is an example of a chair with dark wood and a light cushion. Place it right under the source of gentle light, without any obvious shadows, so that the tones are in the colour of the chair rather than in any light falling on it.

You can put down a few outline dots, but don't connect them up – they are just there to help you see the chair on the space of the paper.

Find the darkest tones in the structure and put them in with the charcoal. Rough the area in and don't try to make the outline too clean.

Then look for the places that are almost as dark, no matter where they are on the structure. Put those in with a slightly lighter touch on the charcoal.

Now look for the whitest or palest places; you want to leave these completely without tone. Indicate where they are by putting a light tone around them.

The result of these simple steps is a finished

tone drawing. Repeat them over and over again with all sorts of objects, learning to see things in gradations of tone and making sure you work in an even light.

Remember that colours can have all sorts of tones within themselves.

Third step: tones in light on the object

Find a source of strong light from one side or the other – a lamp, a south-facing window, or an open door.

Begin with the dots to give you an indication of where the chair is on the paper.

Remember you are still drawing the object, not the environment, so disregard the shadows on the wall or floor and the self-colouring on the chair.

Look for the darkest shadows formed by the light and block them in. Then look for the next darkest and block those in.

Finally, find the lightest places and draw around them very softly.

Remember that in all cases you might very well have the lightest part just along the edge of the darkest part.

Final step: all together

Start with an outline, then draw in the tones of the colour and the effects of light and shadow. The finished drawing should represent the chair just as you see it.

Finally, you'll need to set the chair in its environment. You can do that with an outline, with tone, or with a variety of approaches.

Note: *So that you can appreciate how time governs what you can do, the main section of the book is divided into projects that are appropriate to the time involved. These projects will encourage you to try different approaches in all the mediums.*

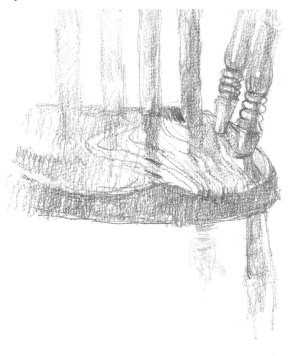

Introduction to watercolour

In some ways, watercolour is the most natural of all painting mediums; the earliest paints were made from clays or tinted earth mixed with a little water. It is also the most flexible tool for the painter, lending itself to almost any artistic purpose.

In watercolour you can render a painting as transparent and light or heavily streaked with primary colours in saturated, brilliant hues. You can draw the most delicate of lines or wash over the entire surface with broad brush-strokes. The paper, too, becomes part of the painting, its texture and tone adding immeasurably to the finished work.

Yet in spite of its immense appeal, watercolour has suffered in the past few centuries from the growth of oil painting, which somehow became the 'serious' medium for gallery artists while watercolour became seemingly inextricably linked in the public mind with preparatory sketches, flower studies and amateur landscape painters.

Today the pendulum is swinging back again. With increasing interest in all the lighter mediums, including pastels, many working artists are using watercolours and gouache again for major paintings, and galleries have discovered that the public enjoys the special appeal and the smaller scale of watercolour paintings, which often give the greatest amount of pleasure for the smallest possible area!

This new esteem and awareness has transformed the leisure market as well; learning to paint is made that much more enjoyable when you have such a delightful medium to work with, needing no more equipment than a box of paints, a brush and a glass of water.

Watercolour paints

Of all the mediums you can use, the quality of the materials is perhaps most important in watercolour. This can be true even if you are working only on light sketches — poor paper will blur the outline of your strokes, muddy colours will reduce the sketch to a scribble, and all the delight and freshness of the medium will be lost.

If you want to prove this for yourself, experiment by buying a single colour — blue is a good choice as it shows up the differences very well — in at least three grades; a cheap children's set, a pan of student quality paint, and a pan or tube of artist's colour. Use a cheap cartridge paper pad, and make two simple washes across the paper, using the children's pan, and the student colour.

Now do the same on a piece of hand-made watercolour paper with a very rough surface, using the artist's colour. Even to the most untrained eye, the difference will be obvious.

When you are buying paints for children, it's as well to remember that little experiment — I feel it is important to give a child at least one box of good colours, even if they also have a large assortment of very cheap brands.

But do look carefully at what you are buying; although in general it is true that you get what you pay for, expensive materials are sometimes sold at highly inflated prices; most colourmen and suppliers have sales from time to time, or special offers, so learn to know what you like to use, and look out for them.

Watercolour paints generally come in two packages; pans and tubes. Both are made up from the same pigment; the pans, being solid, are perhaps easier to carry when you are travelling. The pans are made to fit into standard watercolour boxes, and they also come in two depths, half-pan and full pan.

A fitted box may have the colours already in their pans, but you can move them around as you like, and make up a sequence to suit yourself. The lid usually acts as a palette or mixing area, and with a small brush and a bottle of water, perhaps a few tissues to mop up excess liquid and a sponge to lift off colour, you are completely equipped.

Another benefit of using pans outdoors is that you never use more than you need for one brushstroke, so when you are ready to go home, there is no wasted pigment.

Tube watercolours must be used with a palette, squeezed out in the order you prefer just like oil paints, and you may find at the end of a day spent outdoors that you have too much paint still in blobs on your palette.

However, the texture is thicker and richer, and some artists think the difference is worth the extra trouble involved. Many of us tend to use tubes in the studio, and pans outdoors, thus getting the best of both worlds.

Here are the colours you need for a basic palette:

Cadmium yellow
Yellow ochre
Cadmium red
Alizarin crimson
Burnt umber
Viridian green
Ultramarine blue
Lamp black

When you want to extend your palette, add the following colours:

Lemon yellow
Cadmium orange
Raw sienna
Venetian red
Burnt sienna
Mauve
Hooker's green
Prussian blue
cobalt blue
Vandyke brown
Ivory black

Gouache, tempera and acrylic

There are two other amalgams also used with water, gouache and tempera. Gouache is much denser than watercolour, and is often used with it for highlights or for what is sometimes called body colour; because it is opaque instead of transparent, it is quite useful for adding a little strength to the edge of clouds, or on dark colours for sharp details in the foreground.

Tempera is the watercolour pigment mixed with egg or honey, according to one of the traditional recipes which artists have used since the Middle Ages. It dries very quickly and it makes a surface somewhere between the transparency of watercolour and the opaque covering of gouache. Most suppliers have some tempera in stock colours, but many artists prefer to mix their own from the pigments themselves.

Acrylics are the newest form of paint for the artist, quick-drying, easy to apply, but to my mind at least they do not have the richness or the texture of watercolour or oil paints.

However, they are certainly convenient to use sometimes, and although they are already pre-mixed with a polymer resin binding, they can be diluted with water and used as usual. One benefit is that they take easily to being painted over – the binding keeps the underlayer flat on the paper, instead of lifting as sometimes watercolour pigment can do.

However, they have one real disadvantage – you must wash out your brush as soon as you have finished working; once acrylic dries on a brush it is almost impossible to remove.

Watercolour washes

This is the basic technique of almost all watercolour painting. Once you have learned to lay even and graduated washes, you can start to paint.

Your paper will be pinned to a board, unless it is a very good quality pad which can be used without stretching. Use a full, round brush, with a reasonable quantity of water. Mix in a small amount of the colour, then keeping the board or pad tilted slightly towards you, brush across the entire page in comfortable strokes, starting at the top and working down, laying each stroke across the bottom of the one above, so there is an even covering across the page, and from top to bottom. Once you have finished the page you must let it dry completely before you begin to add anything else.

A graduated wash is usually used for the sky, which naturally pales towards the horizon. Start at the top with a good deal of colour on your brush, then keep adding water without any more colour until at the bottom your strokes are being made with almost no colour at all, just plain water.

Washing out

Washing out is an additional technique for lifting small areas of colour to let the paper show through. After the wash has dried completely, take a small brush, absolutely clean water, and soften the area of the shape you want to remove, and then carefully blot away the colour with the edge of a tissue. Washing out can be used when you want to add clouds to the sky, for example, which had already been laid down across the paper.

Wet on wet

The other basic technique which watercolour artists use a great deal is working wet on wet. The traditional washes were allowed to dry completely before the second layer was added, and the picture was built up in a series of layers, and sometimes glazes as well. But a quite different effect can be achieved by adding washes or details while the first layer is still damp; the edges blur, and make marvellous romantic smudges which are especially fine for distant trees, as in the landscape on the opposite page, or the flower petals in an impressionistic study.

Light areas in the sky, say at sunset or dawn, can also be worked wet on wet.

Working in watercolour

For a first essay in the medium, take your paints and paper with a good quality sketchbook for comfortable working and just start making little pictures of subjects that catch your eye.

Begin at home with a modest subject like this octagonal glass – see how the transparency of the medium has a natural affinity with the transparency of the glass. Look for the sparkle of colour here and there, the reflections inside the base which can be washed on with a few strokes, and the shadows that the glass casts. Don't worry about making the panels absolutely correct – you are looking for an impression of lightness and delicacy.

park lake need only a few strokes each to establish their outline, the angles of their legs, the squatness of the stools. The figures could equally be drawn in charcoal and would have looked much the same.

Now try wet on wet; this simple landscape below is made much more atmospheric by the lovely blurry trees against the soft pink of the winter sun. After the wet on wet strokes were dry, I used a little extra pigment to put in just a few strokes here and there for the main branches. If I had tried to put in too much detail, it would have ruined the effect.

Finally, a detailed view of Venice, below; the sky and foreground were made first with washes and gradually the buildings and their details were added layer by layer, each being allowed to dry for at least half an hour before the next layer was added.

Move out into the park and see if you can use watercolour this time as a drawing medium; these fishermen at the edge of the

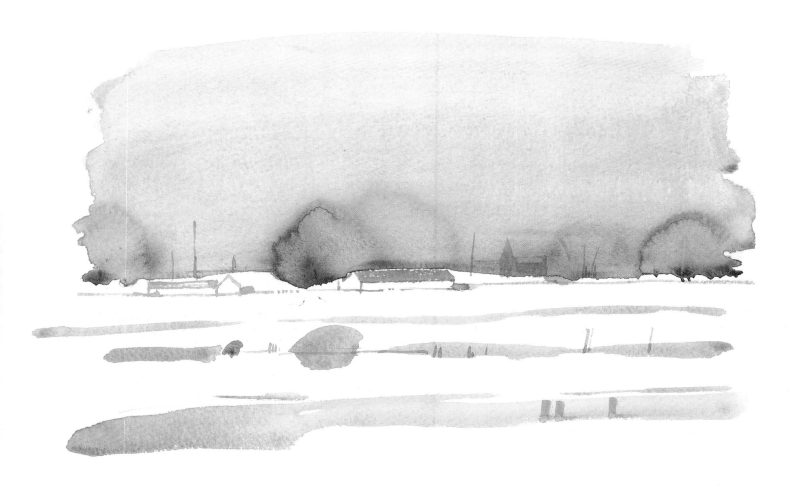

Introduction to oil painting

The youngest of painting mediums dates back to the early 15th century. The favourite tool of medieval artists had been watercolour and tempera; both dry very quickly, requiring a fast eye and hand, as well as speed of reaction, on the part of the artist; there is little or no time to make changes, to experiment and explore. Oil as a binder seemed to give a greater flexibility in creating rich colours, deep shadows, subtle tone on tone, a sheen on the finished canvas, and the chance to alter and correct as the painting develops.

Early paintings in the West were either miniatures in illuminated manuscripts or religious works of art for a particular place in a church, either as an altarpiece on a wood base or on the wall as a fresco. The Flemish painters, such as Jan van Eyck (c. 1384–1441) and Rogier van der Weyden (1399–1464), began to use linseed oil as a binder for the pigments, giving themselves a chance to paint in detailed backgrounds and textures over a long period. They still used wood panels as a base.

The demand grew for private commissions – portraits, in particular, as well as religious paintings for chapels in the home – and portability became important. It is widely accepted that the Flemish painters introduced oil pigments to their Italian contemporaries and that the latter, with the damper climate in the north of the country, especially in Venice, and the resultant problems of cracking and flaking plaster in their frescoes, pioneered the use of canvas as a ground; it has many advantages, especially durability, lightness and texture for the paint to cling to.

By the time of Leonardo da Vinci (1452–1519) and Titian (c.1490–1576), oil had ousted watercolour and tempera as the accepted medium for an artist's greatest work. Although in the most recent decades there has been a return to an appreciation of watercolour and the few artists who work once again in tempera, oil painting remains today the most important technique in a gallery artist's vocabulary, and to many viewers the most satisfying medium because of its endless variety in texture and surface.

Equipment

There is a great deal of paraphernalia in the studio when an artist works with oil paints. You will need a place to keep everything and, above all, a place where paintings can slowly dry without being disturbed – a process which can take not only weeks but even months.

To begin with, a studio easel is useful. If it is sturdy and firm, taking canvases up to 5 ft (1.5 m), you will be able to work sitting down or standing up, depending on your preference, and the canvas can be attacked as vigorously as you like without danger of it flying to the floor. However, since painting away from the one place is also important, if you can only afford one easel buy a travelling model, which can fold up into a relatively small case. Look for the sturdiest kind, though – some are so light that although they are much easier to carry around they have sacrificed stability to that end, and you can find it impossible to apply the brush energetically without everything collapsing.

You will need a sturdy table in the studio, too. Again, size is not important, but it must be stable, standing without rocking back and forth. An old chest of drawers is good; you can use the top for all your equipment when you are painting, and the drawers for storage. Many small drawers are better than a few large ones, but you can always add trays on sliding runners to give you three or four layers in the same drawer.

The next requirement is at least two heavy jars for cleaning and for turpentine. Be careful of plastic – the solvent is sometimes strong enough to make the plastic soften, and in any case they are so light that they can be knocked over all too easily. Try to find old stone jars with large flat bottoms or glass preserving jars. Whatever you use, make sure they are scrupulously clean before you add the liquids.

You'll need somewhere to store your paintings while you are working and after they are finished; on page 116 you will find a project for building a storage rack. This can be anywhere in the house, although it is useful to have it near where you work so that you can look at what you have done from time to time and remind yourself of mistakes – and successful effects.

Try to cover the floor with some sort of inexpensive linoleum or a very old piece of carpet. Unless you work on tiny miniatures, it is impossible to keep oils from spattering.

Brushes and palette knives are discussed on pages 34 and 96 respectively, canvas and priming on page 60. However, you can work perfectly well on hardboard or plywood, which are much cheaper than canvas; you will need to batten large pieces to make them stable, and to sandpaper the surface to give a key for the primer to adhere to properly.

Most oil pigments are bought ready-made; indeed, there is such an assortment at the artist's supplier that the newcomer will be totally confused. However, mixing your own colours is an important part of understanding the medium, so begin with the basics;

White, either titanium or flake
Cadmium yellow
Yellow ochre
Cadmium red
Alizarin crimson
Burnt umber
Viridian green
Ultramarine blue
Ivory black

Once you have learned how to use each of these, exploring the various mixes you can achieve, then you can use an extended palette by adding the following;

Lemon yellow
Deep ochre
Purple
Indian red
Light green
Raw sienna
Raw umber
Cerulean blue
Cobalt blue
Lamp black

Prussian blue is a wonderful colour, but it should be used with great caution as it has a tendency to bleed into other colours around it. Some mixed colours are also very fugitive — that is, they will fade sooner or later and change colour, perhaps affecting the whole painting. The art supply catalogue should tell you which ones to avoid.

Paint in tubes is already mixed with a small amount of oil to help it flow; you add pure turpentine to make it thinner and give greater coverage. Never use turpentine substitute or white spirit for painting — there are often impurities in it which can seriously affect the colour of your paint.

Using a good deal of added turpentine will give you a thin wash which can be laid over a large area just like watercolour. If you use the pigment straight from the tube you will have a thick, rich colour that can be piled up to give a very rough and scumbled surface.

Linseed oil can also be used to extend the paint, but it should be added sparingly; these mixes are called 'fatter' while turpentine-thinned mixes are 'leaner'. I begin painting with very lean mixes, opaque and almost filmy, as the background, moving to richer colours and deeper texture of oily mixes on the surface. If you use the fatter layers on the base, they will almost certainly crack.

Linseed also has a tendency to yellow some of the colours, and most painters use poppy oil when working in the lighter pigments; either can be useful when you have decided to go back to work on a painting which has already dried out. Brush the pure oil over the surface, wipe off any that does not sink in, and leave it for a few minutes. The surface becomes soft again, and you can recommence work. It is also used after a painting has dried as a kind of varnish to lift the colours which may have darkened and dulled. Another useful trick is to keep adding a very light coat of retouching varnish over the layers as they dry out, so that each layer keeps fresh and bright.

There are drying gels now in most stores which are very useful if you are in a hurry to finish — either working outdoors or for an exhibition. They will affect the colour eventually, so use them with caution.

Working with oil

Oil is a most flexible medium which can be used by the artist with almost every technique imaginable. You can, as noted, thin it so much that you can wash it on with large brushes. Slightly thicker, it can be layered, tone on tone, also in the traditional watercolour technique, waiting until each layer is dry before you paint over it. Thus a painting can be finished in weeks, months, or even years. The great advantage is that oil is opaque, so that each layer can completely cover what is beneath. When you want the transparency of the old master style, then you add a little glazing varnish to the paint — it will give a warm glow to anything beneath.

In the alla prima technique, the paint is handled quite differently; wet paint is worked into and on to wet paint, and the work must be completed before the paint dries, usually a matter of a day or two at the most. Nonetheless, you can call on the ability of oil to return to fundamentals; if you come back to a painting during the day and find you really don't like what you have done in one corner, you can scrape off the pigment right back to the primer and start again. It is a very forgiving medium, and knowing you can change your mind is a soothing possibility when you are discouraged or disappointed.

The flourish of alla prima was used by Titian

and other old masters; today it has been adapted to the most outré of modern techniques – pigment is blown, sprayed, dribbled, moulded, applied with trowels, fingers, or whatever tool the artist fancies. It can also result in the most delicate art, with fine detailing and tiny images as clear as the work of a miniaturist.

When you begin to paint with oils, don't stop at one technique – learn to experiment, to try out all sorts of ideas and methods, using different bases and different shapes of canvas. Never be afraid to change something and explore new ways of working; its versatility is, perhaps, the medium's greatest contribution to our vocabulary of art.

Left, oil is particularly suited to unusual modern techniques, such as this spatter paint panel. Try making different patterns for yourself with drips, spatters, splashes.

When you put away brushes for long-term storage, remember that painting in oils always requires a greater variety of brushes than watercolour; you will probably need to find a specific kind of brush quite often, so sort the different types of brush into separate boxes. This way you needn't unpack three or four layers before you find what you want.

Right, here are two panels of seasonal colours; these are the most useful colours for me throughout the years.

Spring:
Pale lemon
Pale yellow ochre
Raw sienna
Cobal blue
Viridian green
Cadmium red

Summer:
Cadmium yellow
Yellow ochre
Burnt umber
Ultramarine blue
Viridian green
Cadmium red

Autumn:
Cadmium yellow deep
Yellow ochre
Burnt umber
Alizarin crimson
Ultramarine blue
Viridian green
Lamp black

Winter:
Yellow ochre
Raw umber
Prussian blue
Cobalt blue
Alizarin crimson
Viridian green
Ivory black

30-Minute Projects

1. Quick sketches indoors
2. The care, maintenance and storage of brushes
3. Stretching paper for watercolour
4. Composition for a still life painting
5. Laying out an oil palette
6. Working with a viewing card
7. Keeping a diary
8. Experimenting with light
9. Making a colour wheel
10. Using a camera

Tom Robb

1. Quick sketches indoors

In the introduction there are many suggestions on how to experiment with the materials an artist uses in order to discover what paint and pencils can and cannot do. Now, in the space of just a brief half-hour during the day or in the evening, you can begin by drawing simple things that you see around you in the house.

To make a study for a still life, choose a few things that are interesting but not too complicated; introductory projects usually feature an apple and a bottle, but something a little more adventurous can still be simple to do while being a little more effective as a drawing. A tall vase has colour and form, without any hard edges. Add a smaller vase, a few plates, a red pepper, a potato and a cup; put them all on a small table and the result is just right, a natural grouping of some things you might put down casually when you are getting ready for dinner.

Working to a timetable means that it is important to have everything to hand. Spend just a few minutes gathering up all your equipment, as well as the props, before you begin.

Equipment

A small area to sit down and work in
A table about 4–5 ft (1.2–1.5 m) away from your chair
A sketchbook (A3 or A4) of heavy cartridge paper
A set of felt-tip pens, or a box of pastels or watercolours. If you choose pastels you will need fixative
The objects; in the example, a few household objects put down quickly, without worrying too much about the arrangement

Start with a single outline of everything in light grey so that you fix the individual pieces on to the page. Work very quickly – that way you will actually have a better chance of filling the paper than if you try too hard to judge the relative sizes and shapes or work too long on each outline independently.

Next draw each object, using the nearest appropriate colour. Begin with the lightest colour first. Making blocks of colour like this will create an almost abstract composition.

Now add shadows, details and highlights. Keep working quickly without trying to be too accurate. Look at one detail at a time; the diamond pattern on the smaller vase, for example. Fix the object in your mind, look down and make the marks you need. Then look at the vase again just to check quickly that you have more or less the correct position and colour. Move on to the next detail at once – the round shadows under the plates. Look at these, find the right colour and draw them in immediately. Go on working from detail to detail, keeping the general effect as free and as light as you can.

When you have finished, let it dry. If you have used pastels, spray lightly with fixative or there will be nothing left in half an hour – the picture will be on your hands instead of on the paper!

Putting the pastels back into the box in the right order helps to teach your hand where every colour is and you will be able to reach for the one you want even while your eyes are watching the fleeting highlight on a sunlit flower.

This way of working from detail to detail is not necessarily the method you would use when you have more time; it is a painter's shorthand to teach your eye to take in as much as possible in as brief a time as possible.

Note: If you run over 30 minutes, don't go on until you finish. Stop and start again when you have another 30 minutes free. Learning the discipline of working quickly is very important. Next time, use an egg timer or an alarm so you can pace yourself and make sure you don't spend the whole half-hour on one russet streak of one apple!

More suggestions for quick sketches indoors:

Do a group in each room in the house; a few things on the bathroom sink, a bedside table with a lamp and a book, the inside of the kitchen cupboard, and so on.

Looking beyond still-life groupings can produce a lot of potential subjects – for example, shutters on the window, a landscape through the door, a bookcase of bright jackets, inside your wardrobe, children's toys . . .

Try to do at least one sketch every day. It will give you not only enormous pleasure but also a great deal of gradually accumulated experience in seeing objects quickly but accurately.

2. The care, maintenance and storage of brushes

The major cause of deterioration of brushes, aside from natural wear, is neglect by the painter, who usually commits one of these primary mistakes:

1. Working against the way the bristles are set and breaking the hairs
2. Leaving the brushes clogged with paint
3. Failing to store the brushes carefully

Brushes should never be used as if they were paint stirrers. Even mixing paints on the palette or canvas must be done in small amounts and with a light touch; a scrubbing motion will break off the filaments, disturb their set in the handle, and generally make a mess of them. Use a palette knife, an old brush, or even a small, clean stick instead.

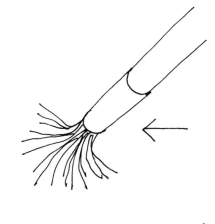

Putting the paint on canvas or paper also needs a light hand. Always use the brush in a straight line with the direction of the handle and never push the hairs around; brushes are delicate instruments, as fragile as a fine pen.

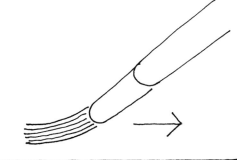

The principle of painting technique is to use the brush to lift the paint from the palette and put it on the canvas; it is not necessary to cover the entire brush with paint right up to the ends of the hairs where they meet the metal ferrule. All the paint you need at one time can be carried on the tip.

Try painting simple strokes in various directions with different brushes.

The worst sin is to let paint dry on the brush. With rare exceptions, once this has been done two or three times the point and the suppleness of the hairs are lost forever.

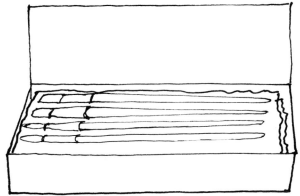

Cleaning

There are two basic kinds of paint: water based and oil based. The water-based paints include:

    acrylic
    tempera
    gouache
    watercolour

If acrylic dries on the hairs, forget it. Throw away the brush.

Tempera and gouache can be dissolved by a long soaking in water and detergent. Rinse in clear water, wash out with ordinary soap and water, then rinse again. Gently squeeze the water out of the brushes so that the sables come to a point and flat hogs to a chisel edge, then stand upright to dry.

Watercolour is the only pigment that can be easily washed off, even after it has dried out, with clean water.

The oil-based paints include:

    oil
    alkalyd

If the pigment has only just dried, try soaking it in white spirit to soften it, leaving it overnight. If it has been left for any period of time, detergent powder (a couple of spoonfuls) mixed with hot water into a creamy paste is a good solution; stand the brush in it, tied to a stick, and leave until the paint has dissolved. In this one case, the bristles are so stiff with paint that standing the brush on them won't do any damage. This treatment may take weeks or even months, but it should eventually work. Rinse in clean water and stand upright to dry.

Alternatively, you can use a large can of turpentine, with a layer of wire mesh about halfway up the can. The hairs are cleaned by being brushed gently back and forth on the mesh, dislodging the pigment, which falls to the bottom while the top of the turpentine clears. The advantage of this method is that the bristles are not damaged during cleaning. You can use the same turpentine until it is too dirty to clear overnight.

When you are out painting, clean oil brushes with white spirit and wrap them in a cloth until you can get home to wash them as suggested above. Alternatively, wrap them very tightly in cling film so that they stay damp until you can clean them; wipe excess paint off before you start cleaning them.

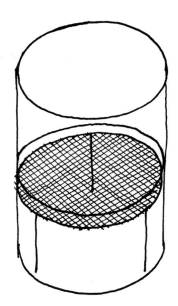

Regular maintenance

Hog brushes that splay out and fray can be put back into shape by a weak solution of size — about two tablespoons to a pint of hot water. Dip the brush in, shake it out and bring it to a point with your fingers. Stand it upright and when it is completely dry brush it lightly back and forth to restore its shape.

Another method is to dampen the brush lightly, then drag it gently over a warm iron, a hot-water pipe, a radiator or a hot towel rail. This expands the bristles and they curl into shape.

Watercolour brushes need only be washed under running water, shaken out, shaped to a point and left upright in a jar to dry.

You must tidy up individual bristles or hairs that won't go back into shape; dragging hairs may well ruin a finely drawn detail. Cut these back to the edge of the ferrule using a razor blade or a pair of fine scissors.

Remove paint regularly from ferrules and handles. You can use a proprietary paint stripper if the colours have really become hardened, but work very carefully; you must never get paint stripper on the handle or the hairs, so it is better to rely on scraping and scrubbing if this will suffice.

If you are really tidy by nature you can repaint the ends of worn handles by dipping them in paint and hanging them up on a line, held by a clothes peg clipped to the ferrule. Keep a newspaper underneath to catch the drips. It will keep them looking smart and fresh and you can colour-code or initial the handles, too — especially useful if you are a student or in some kind of art class where your things are likely to get mixed up with other students' material.

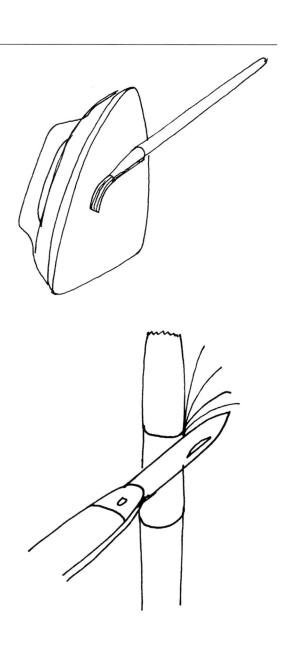

Storing brushes

Signwriters have been known to store their brushes in oil. Use a can of stand oil, which never dries. The brushes must never rest on the bottom; hold them with a clothes peg or drill a hole through them at the point of balance and then suspend them from a wire.

Short-term storage

During normal periods of time between use (i.e. up to a few months) brushes can simply be kept upright in a convenient mug or vase. Short brushes should be together in a short vase, long brushes in a taller one. This is not just for aesthetic effect – long brushes will tend to topple over in a small vase, and short brushes will get lost in a tall one!

Store your brushes away from sticks of chalk, pastels, charcoal and other bits and pieces or they will become sticky and dirty.

Long-term storage

There are a number of circumstances in which you may find that some brushes need to be put away for a considerable length of time – for example, if moving house or going away for a long holiday. If you are lucky enough to find a really good brush, with a comfortable handle that is a good length for your style of painting and a shape which allows the paint to flow easily, it makes a lot of sense to buy a few extra and put them away. Cheap man-made fibre brushes won't be affected by moths or damp, but they also won't provide the same technical skill and they don't last nearly as well. Brushes are getting more expensive every year, and some kinds of hair are no longer even available. The best long-haired hog bristle from Russia and China is almost non-existent now because the animals themselves have been replaced by more modern breeds, and Russian sable, for example, is being priced completely out of the market. The purchase twenty years ago of a hundred long-haired brushes would have been a very worthwhile investment indeed.

Perhaps you have also acquired paint kits over the years with brushes that you don't use, but which you should not throw away. Sometimes a change of medium means you have a set of equipment to put aside.

Any brushes to be stored should be absolutely clean and dry. Clean them as suggested on p.34 then dry them standing upright, possibly putting them in a warm place for a few hours to make sure all excess moisture has gone.

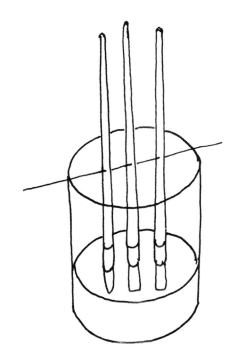

If they are new, remove any elastic bands or non-acid paper. Remember that you should only wrap brushes in acid-free tissue.

Lay the brushes flat. You want to exclude all air if you can so find a box of appropriate size, making absolutely sure that there is enough room for the tips without bending them. If there are more than two or three layers, lay them top to tail alternately so that they stay evenly in layers.

Leave room in the box for moth and insect balls. Remember that there are grubs, spiders, mites, carpet beetles and so on that adore wood and hair. You must also include one damp-absorbing ball or sachet of crystals; they are easily available from supermarkets and ironmongery stores. Some are colour-coded so that when they are full or no longer effective they change colour. In any case, check up on the brushes every six months or so, change the damp sachets if necessary and make sure all is well.

After the brushes are packed, tape the box up so that the air is excluded and put on a dated label with the contents clearly marked; add the date each time you check them and you'll have an invaluable record.

3. Stretching paper for watercolour

The purpose of stretching paper is to make sure that when you use water as part of your medium the paper will lie flat, rather than curling up at the edges and ruining the finished work.

Heavier papers can sometimes be used without stretching – pads often consist of really heavy paper that you can work on just as it comes. However, for the best results, all paper that will have water applied to it should be stretched first as, once it has wrinkled, it's never possible to render it flat again.

Begin by making sure you have a flat board. A drawing board or a piece of marine plywood or good-quality hardboard will do; it must be unaffected by water and at least 2 inches (5 cm) larger all round than the paper you are stretching.

All paper has two surfaces – a working or top surface that will give you a better painting sheet, and a back. In a bound pad the working surface will lie on top, so make sure as you take it out that you keep it that side up.

The most obvious clue to establishing the top surface is the watermark; it should read correctly. On any hand-made sheet, with or without a mark, there are likely to be light lines on the back left by the wire mesh of the tray where the paper was dried; hold the paper up to the light at an angle to see them.

Much of the machine-made paper used today, however, has no obvious back or front, and it will not matter whether you stretch it the right way up or not because there will not be much of a difference when you come to paint.

Dampen the sheet of paper lightly on both sides with a sponge by laying the paper on top of the board and wiping it *evenly* from top to bottom and side to side; there must not be more water on one area than another. Start on the back, or wrong, side, then turn the paper over and work on the top.

Make sure you don't scrub the sponge into the paper or you might find yourself with a paper full of holes. Uneven sponging will make the sheet lopsided, with dry areas left unstretched and wrinkles everywhere else.

Once the paper is prepared on both sides, lay it back on the board with the painting surface on top ready for taping. Gummed paper strip is the easiest tape to use; the narrow strips are best for small sheets, the wider strips for large. Cut off a strip a little longer than the length of the sheet. Run it quickly under the tap, dunk it in a bowl of water, or sponge it down; then simply tape the paper to the board quickly, making sure it lies absolutely flat. Repeat on all four sides. It is essential that the paper be evenly stretched across its length and width or it will buckle.

Allow the paper to dry in normal room temperature; leave it overnight at least. If you try to use artificial heat of any kind the paper is likely to split.

As soon as it is dry you can work on it in the usual way, with the paper still taped to the board. It will have dried absolutely flat. After you have finished painting let it dry again, then, using a scalpel or knife, cut it off the board just inside the line of tape. Strip the tape off the board, and you are ready to start again. If you enjoy watercolour painting it is useful to do quite a few sheets at once and keep them stacked up on their boards until you need them. You can work on both sides of the board as long as you are careful when painting not to dirty the other side.

All these papers are made from pure cotton rag and they are all acid-free, which means that they won't fade, or alter the colours you put on them. They can also be used for printmaking and drawing. Although it is possible in an emergency to use the heavier papers or the block papers without stretching them it is still advisable that all papers, no matter what texture or weight, be stretched for the best results. You can see from the photograph that none of them, even the papers which are so heavy they are more like card, lie absolutely flat, and so your painting is bound to be affected.

1. Machine-made paper with a machine texture, from a watercolour block. It has a regular, somewhat dimpled pattern. The edge is absolutely straight, having been trimmed just like any notepaper or typing paper.

2. First HOT press, or smooth surfaced, hand-made paper, of a fairly light weight. It is ironed when wet to give it a smooth texture.

3. Same as above but heavyweight, i.e. twice as thick. Heavy paper can be used without stretching for watercolour. Both of these papers have a natural hand-made edge, but as they are thinner than No 4 the edge does not turn back and the deckling is not very evident.

4. Heavy hand-made paper with a rougher surface called NOT (usually interpreted as NOT IRONED). The edge has been left as it comes off the tray so that it curls back in a natural deckle.

5. A very heavy machine-made paper with a rough texture but a straight machine-cut edge. It is cheaper than the hand-made papers but is good quality and, aside from the irregularities in texture, it serves as well as a hand-made paper of the same quality.

6. A very heavy, rough, hand-made paper, with a real deckle edge characterized by the natural irregularities of a thinning edge running out of the paper area and turning back slightly as the sheet is lifted from the screen.

7. A similar paper, but extremely heavy, with a rough texture; the heaviest paper of all.

8. A heavy machine-made paper with an artificial deckle edge put on by a mechanical process of feathering.

9. A lightweight machine-made paper. This is often called Bank Note paper; very strong, it is also used in book binding. This must be carefully stretched, when it becomes extremely tight and flat. After painting or drawing the sheets are usually mounted over another layer of white paper for opacity.

10. Waterleaf paper; this resembles a blotting paper. Pure cotton rag, with a very low size content, it cannot be stretched, or drawn on with a pen, nor can any marks be erased. Only for large, soft washes, it is particularly nice for working wet on wet.

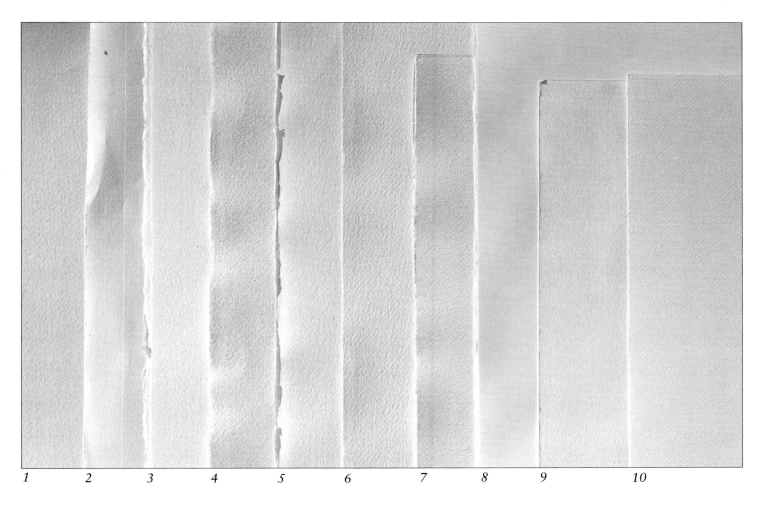

1   2   3   4   5   6   7   8   9   10

4. Composition for a still-life painting

Planning the time for making a thoughtful still-life painting is easier if you break up some of the preparation into smaller periods. When you know that, for example, you will be able to set aside a morning or even a day on a painting at the weekend, you can save your precious painting time by finding just the right composition beforehand, trying out a number of different ideas at your leisure.

First Study

Forget about individual objects that might be important in themselves. Look for pattern, colour and shape; this is going to be a study in one picture plane, the composition based on the total effect without reference to the objects in 'real' life. There are many still lifes by Cézanne, for instance, where a jug is tilted up on the table so that the line along the rim becomes an open ellipse.

Start with background material – a table-cloth, a scarf or a particularly nice polished wood surface with an interesting grain. You'll find that you start looking for fabric and wallpaper remnants in a variety of tone, colour and pattern to provide just such backgrounds. Remember that this will be the dominant feature in the picture, so it should be chosen first.

Put the background material on the table or drape it on the wall and start to gather together the other objects you will need.

Add as much variety as you can. Don't restrict yourself to the obvious, solid objects around you; think about texture and colour. Try crumpled tissue or kitchen roll paper, or a handful of leaves.

Walk around the house quickly, observing its contents; it helps to teach your eye to see beyond the meaning of an object to its fundamental position in space. Pick up lots of things, and carry them back to your background.

Put the objects in place, trying to see them as shapes related to each other, so that they are not spread out evenly without touching (that usually makes for a boring picture) or piled up on one side so that nothing really registers.

Make sure you have objects of different shapes and put them in different positions; some flat, some standing, some round, some square. They need not have any relation to each other – you are simply making a collection of things that please your eye.

You'll need things that blend together, and one final object to give real punch; if your objects are in dark, rich colours, try one white handkerchief or a brilliant yellow cup. If the colours are all pastel and flowery, then a red billiard ball or a luscious apple will make the right impact.

Second Study

This is a composition for a traditional still life; that is, it includes a setting for the objects. In contrast to the first sketch, you are trying to build a picture that is based on recognition – the ingredients of a meal, a bouquet of flowers, a corner of a room.

Start with the background, still the dominant colour (unless you fade it away at the edges). Then collect the objects that reflect your theme on the background, remembering to look for variety in shape, texture and colour.

The same principles of distribution on the canvas still apply; a picture with everything equally apart will generally look boring, and you need a focal point, in colour as well as shape. So that final touch is vital – a single, fully open scarlet rose, a huge cabbage in brilliant green, or a yellow cushion on a chair.

Variety does not have to mean violently different. An armful of leaves will have a hundred different shades of green and brown, and you could paint a very subtle still life in tones of one colour – but make sure you have plenty of textures.

Keep the objects within a reasonable space either on a table or in a corner of the room. Paintings which take in a very large area have their own particular problems.

5. Laying out an oil palette

Putting your colours on the palette in an appropriate sequence is not just an exercise in making your work look photogenic. It is intended to help you work faster, and to guide your brush to the right colour quickly and accurately.

There is no absolute format for your palette, but it should have its own inherent rationale.

One system is based on white being in the middle, with cool colours to one side, warm to the other.

My own preference is based on the one Cézanne used, generally referred to as the Impressionist palette. This goes, right to left, white, lemon yellow, cadmium yellow, yellow ochre, cadmium red, Indian red, alizarin crimson, raw sienna, burnt sienna, raw umber, burnt umber, viridian, cerulean blue, cobalt blue, ultramarine, Prussian blue, black. The colours are standard, but Cézanne used his colours in blocks (see overleaf).

This is fairly extensive and it is perfectly acceptable to use a smaller number of colours, especially if you are painting outdoors; try white, cadmium yellow, yellow ochre, cadmium red, alizarin crimson, burnt umber, viridian, ultramarine and black; these colours would be quite enough for normal use.

Most artists work from left to right, and from dark to light, but some, particularly left-handed painters, prefer to work the other way around.

The rationale for this particular arrangement is that white is the basic colour, and you will be using it most frequently in order to make light tints; if you are right-handed, placing white first will put it nearest to your brush. The yellows are the next lightest colours, then into the darker, warm colours, the reds, from the lighter cadmium to alizarin, then to the still deeper browns. The palette moves on to the cool colours of blue and then to the darkest of all, black. Green is a neutral colour, neither cool nor warm, so it sits comfortably in between the browns and blues.

Of course, there are specialized arrangements; portrait painters, for example, have individual mixtures of colours in yellows and pinks for flesh tints. Working on a bowlful of red roses, it would be quite difficult to mix all your red tints on the canvas, so the sensible flower painter buys a much wider range of reds; colours such as carmine, rose madder, mauve and purple are available ready to use. There are many useful greens, too, at the colourman's – Hooker's green, sap green, cadmium green, cobalt green, and so on.

Once you have gained personal experience in how colours mix together, then using these additional ready-mixed colours will really help to add sparkle and clarity to your palette and save valuable painting time. However, do be warned – if you tried to buy and carry every colour in the art materials shop you would need wheels just for your paintbox. Learn to use a minimal palette first, then add only those colours that are especially suitable for the kind of painting in which you want to specialize.

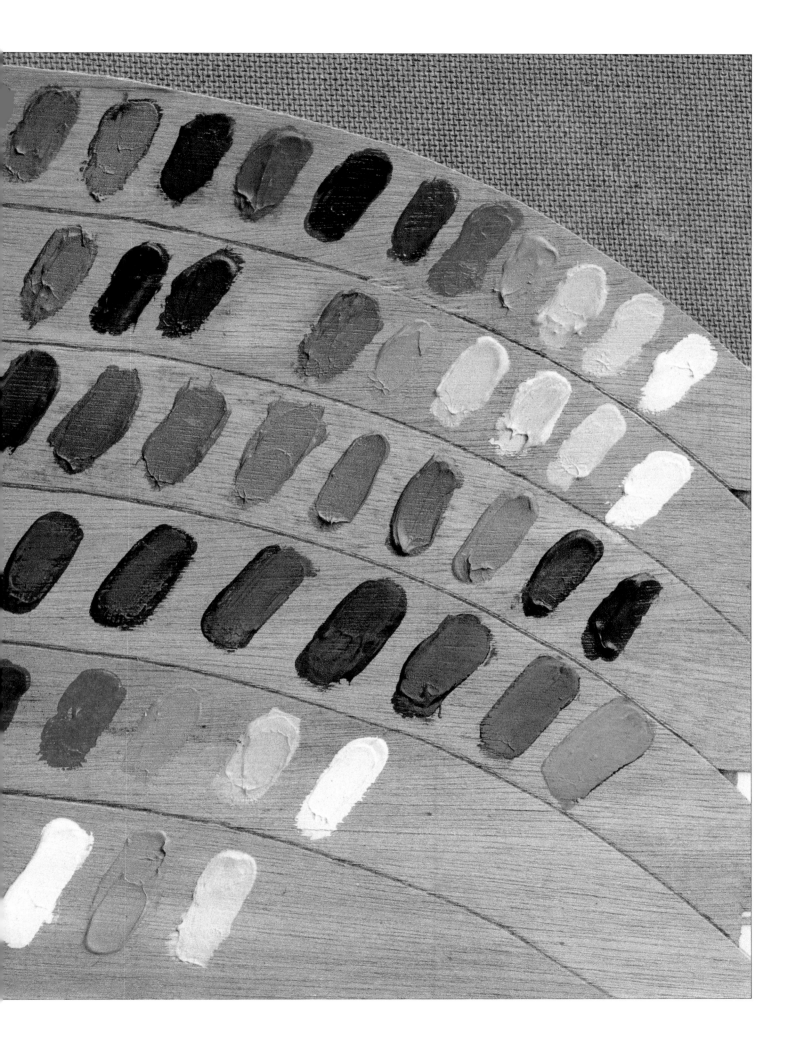

6. Working with a Viewing Card

When you are confronted by the huge expanse of a landscape it can be totally bewildering. What on earth do you choose to paint? Where are the ends of your painting? How can you find that one small area which it is possible to put down on your relatively small canvas? As in all things, experience will help your eye to isolate the piece of the whole which interests you.

However, there is a simple aid which anyone can make. A viewing card is the ideal solution; it makes a frame for the countryside, restricting your eye and helping you to find the particular place you want to paint.

Start with a piece of black card; mark out one square shape and one of a square and a half (see diagram). They need not be more than $2\frac{1}{8} \times 2\frac{1}{8}$ inches (53×53 mm) and $2\frac{1}{8} \times 3$ inches (53×76 mm).

These will give you the most popular shapes, but if you prefer to paint on canvases that are a different shape, alter your viewing cards accordingly.

If you really want to have a flexible system, make two 'L' shapes in card; they can be held together with clips or bits of tape and adjusted to an infinite number of sizes. You can see on the spot what happens to the composition if you lengthen or shorten one of the sides, perhaps to include a particularly magnificent tree or exclude an awful building.

When you hold your viewing card close to your eye you will be able to see the entire panorama; if you hold it at arm's length, you may just be able to see that one tree!

Try swinging it around with the sun in front of you, behind you, or to one side, so you see how the views are affected by shadow and sunlight.

You can also adjust the amount of sky in your paintings, holding the card up or down to keep the horizon high or low.

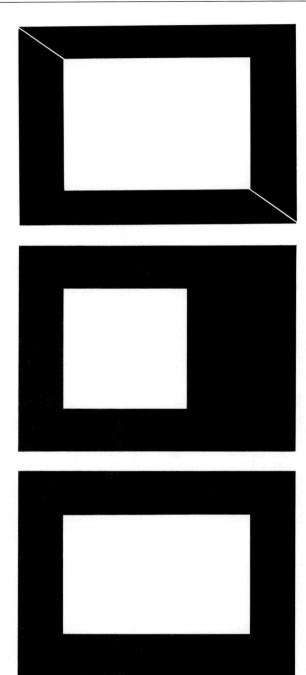

7. Keeping a diary

Art is an accumulation of craftsmanship and inspiration, and there is no better way to encourage both of these elements than to keep a careful diary of your work and your progress as a painter.

On the most practical level, it is important to know how long individual pictures took to paint, how often you needed to buy new pigments, brushes, or paper (very useful indeed when you see items on sale) and what you paid for them.

There is also the element of self-assessment; a record of each day's work bearing witness to the fact that although you say you prefer to paint outdoors you actually do it mostly indoors, and at night at that, should lead to some careful re-organization!

If, as it is for most of us, your free time is at weekends, your dairy may show that very little work is done because of constant interruptions from family, friends and telephone calls, or for necessary shopping expeditions. In order to produce a piece of work for a commission or an exhibition it might be necessary to get out of the house to paint if it is to be finished on time; alternatively, you'll have to set aside more time in the evenings, especially in the spring and summer when the light is still good until late in the day.

Forward planning is another benefit of keeping a diary; for example, note down when you will need new frames for an exhibition, or the time for a visit to the local art gallery for a special show.

To incorporate all these elements, including notes about pictures you are working on, problems you might have encountered and points to remember, it's best to buy a large, inexpensive page-a-day diary, ideally unlined so you can add little drawings here and there.

Right: A sample which could have come from one of my diaries; on Sunday I intended to go out painting but it rained all day, so I went on Monday instead. The extra space was useful for making notes the night before.

MAY

1 Sunday
Week 17 · 122-244

things to check the evening before you go. All art materials in bag, Money, cheque book, rain coat, sun hat, tickets, maps

Places of interest if it rains: Art Gallery, Regency houses, Museum, local church, Places to draw from if it is wet: Bus or rail station, cafe, church, any covered area – doorways.

May

Sun	Mon Tue Wed Thu Fri Sat Sun	Mon Tue Wed Thu Fri Sat Sun	Mon Tue Wed Thu Fri Sat Sun	Mon Tue Wed Thu Fri Sat Sun	Mon Tue
1	2 3 4 5 6 7 8	9 10 11 12 13 14 15	16 17 18 19 20 21 22	23 24 25 26 27 28 29	30 31

Divide the page into three sections. Use the top to record any work finished that day; even a group of little sketches can be noted with diagrams. Put down what media you used, and if there was anything particularly successful or difficult that you encountered while you were working – perhaps the white highlights in a portrait, or the first time you used a particular form of glaze or varnish.

Use the second section for special reminders; a picture sold, or sent for framing; the entry form for a group show that needs to be filled in; the date for renewing a subscription to an art magazine.

Finally, use the lowest section as a shopping list; note anything you are using up and will need to replace, or a new product that you saw advertised or heard about from a friend. Cross the notes out when you buy what you need. If you keep this information right at the bottom, you can pick out immediately what still needs to be done on flicking through the diary.

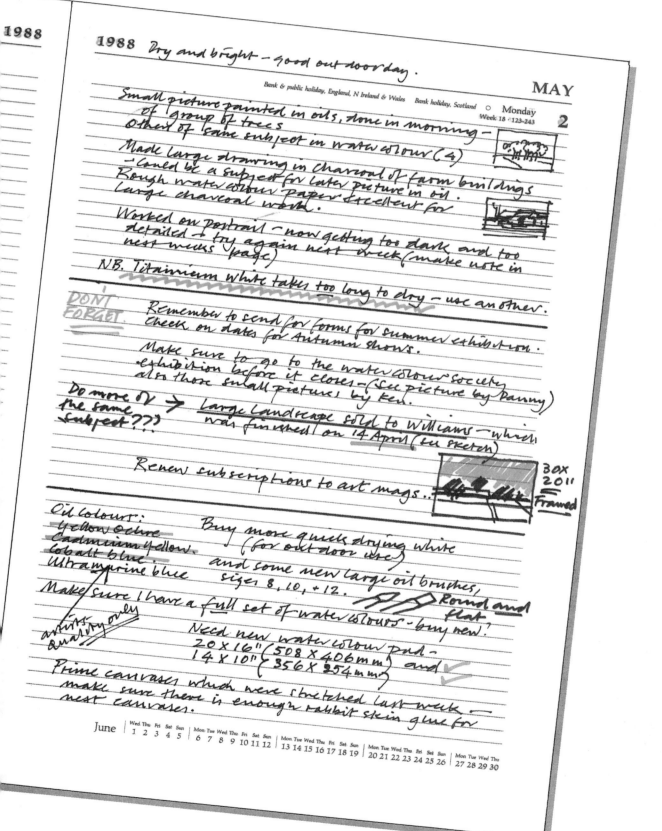

8. Experimenting with light

This is a quick study of how light can radically alter everything you see. Understanding how light behaves is an essential part of good composition.

There are three main sources of light; daylight (including sunlight), ordinary electric light with tungsten bulbs, and so-called 'daylight' fluorescent tubes, which are supposed to imitate the neutral effect of daylight.

Daylight itself can vary enormously from the greyish light of an overcast day, through the neutral tone of a north window to the warm yellow of a bright sun.

Nonetheless, tungsten is warm compared to daylight, even direct sunlight. It will lend a distinctly warm tone to everything and particularly to any objects painted with lamplight falling directly on them.

Daylight tubes are cooler than tungsten, approximating the same colour range as ordinary sunlight, but these are not easy to find with household fittings, and as we are used to tungsten lamps, most of us would find the colour rather cold to live with. However, if you paint indoors often and you have managed to set aside an area you can use regularly as a studio it is certainly worth investing in an electrical fitting on the ceiling that will take a daylight tube.

As well as these basic three sources there are variations that you can make using direct and indirect light: direct light can come from sunlight, or a bare clear bulb; diffused light comes from a pearl bulb, a neon or fluorescent tube, or a cloudy sky, or direct light shielded by a curtain or a translucent shade. Indirect light is only seen refracted from its source; for example, slanting through a window and bouncing off the ceiling or the walls, or thrown up by lights behind pelmets or opaque shades.

Side light

Back light

Low level view

Backlighting, looking into the source of light

Back light

Help yourself to see all these variations by assembling a group of objects on a tray. Make them strong, simple shapes and colours; a white vase, a black box, a bright blue teapot, a large red tomato.

Move the tray around the house, putting it in different positions, for example near a window or on the floor. Try it on different sides of the house to appreciate the difference between north light, south light, and so on. You can discern some of the light variation in a photograph, but the eye is far more subtle and sees all kinds of nuances in colour that will not register on any four-colour process film.

Dark back light

Medium back light

If you become really interested in this kind of experimentation, make this 30-minute project into a day's work! Try to paint colour studies with the tray standing in different kinds of light. I promise you'll be amazed at how different the same objects appear once you begin to look carefully at them under varied light sources — and if you can paint a blue teapot in sunlight, indoors under a lamp or by an open window, then you can paint anything, anywhere!

Light back light

51

9. Making a colour wheel

This project demonstrates the basis of all colour mixing, and making your own wheel is the very best way to assess exactly how colours relate to each other.

Equipment

A tube each of the following colours;
Cadmium Red
Cobalt Blue
Cadmium Yellow
(Acrylic paint will do very well, being quick to dry and easy to handle; the lack of richness in the texture doesn't really matter.)
A sheet of cartridge paper
A sheet of thin tracing paper

A hard pencil
A very soft pencil
A medium brush

Trace the outline wheel below on to the thin paper with the hard pencil. Rub the soft pencil over the back of the tracing paper in an all-over scribble so that the paper is completely covered.

Gently put the tracing paper, scribbled side down, on to the cartridge paper and go over the outline again with the hard pencil; the pressure will transfer the outline to the cartridge paper beneath. You can write the appropriate colours in the spaces very lightly if you wish.

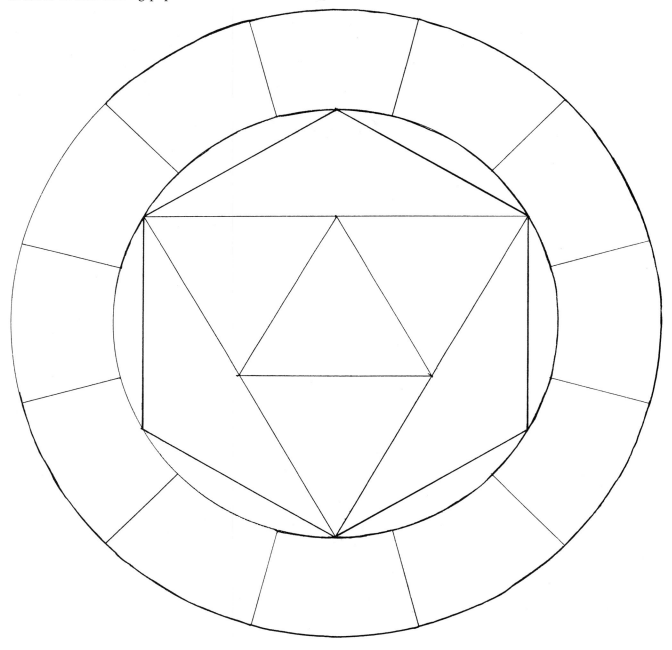

Lay out your paints far apart, so that there is no chance of the colours running into each other on the palette. Using as little water as possible so that the paint doesn't run at all and rinsing the brush carefully after each use, paint in the pure red, yellow and blue triangles in the centre.

These are your primary colours. When you mix two primary colours together you make a secondary colour. You will see that the flat sides of adjoining triangles show which colours are mixed together in equal amounts to make the secondary colours. At the top, yellow and red make orange. On the left, red and blue make violet, and on the right yellow and blue make green.

The point of each primary-coloured triangle is set in the middle of a section of the outer band. Fill in these primary sections first; yellow, red and blue. Now fill in the sections of the band indicated by the points of the secondary triangles, violet, orange, and green.

Remember to clean the brush every time you change colour.

There are six gaps left. These are the tertiary colours, and they are mixed using equal amounts of the colours on either side. They should look as if they were exactly halfway between the two; you may need to practise using equal amounts of each colour on a bit of paper.

Although it seems so straightforward, making an accurate colour wheel can take an hour or more. The important point is to have twelve colours in equal progression around the outer band. If you mix the first secondary colours with too much of one pigment it will affect the progression right around the circle, so take your time and work as slowly as you need to.

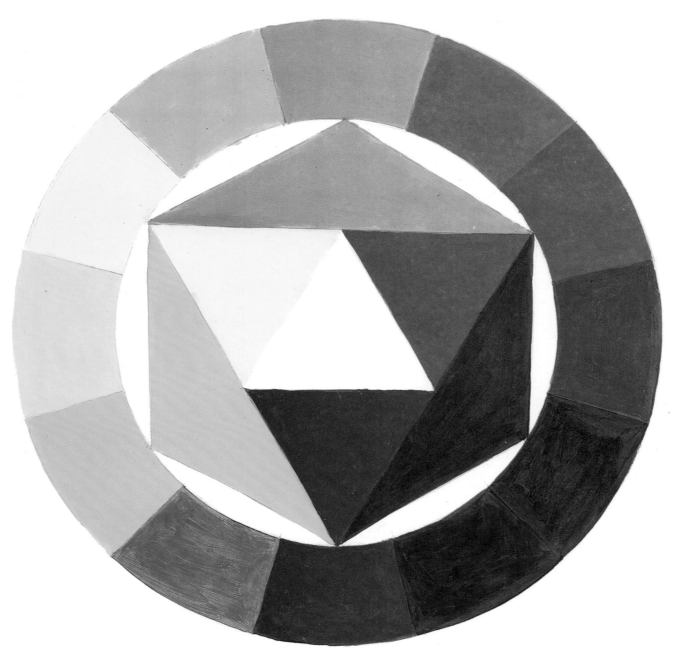

10. Using a camera

Once you begin to see all the subtleties that the eye can discern, then working from colour photographs is like using a blunt instrument, they are really disappointing in the way they are limited to combinations of four crude colours.

However, cameras do have their uses for the artist, and learning to make the most of their possibilities can be fun as well as instructive.

Use colour film to make a record for yourself of everything you paint; even though it won't be accurate, it will be helpful for your diary, and for charting progress towards the development of skill and a personal style. Photograph the paintings outside on a clear sunny day; take them so they fill the whole frame, and you will get as near to the real thing as you can.

Black and white film is often a better way of recording a view or an object; it will give a clear indication of basic shapes and tones, as well as the light source. You can write colour notes on the back if necessary.

I try to keep a note of the progress of long-term projects by taking black and white photographs as I go along. This gives a real sense of development; I've often seen difficulties in composition and drawing that eventually I have had to put right, and which hopefully will be handled better from the beginning next time around. At one time, too, I used a great deal of tonal underpainting in oils, but as I could see from the photographs that it vanished completely from the finished picture the camera saved me hours, even days, of unnecessary effort.

For this project, use good-quality black and white film. Take a painting you are working on – any one you like, as long as it is only half-finished – and photograph it so that it fills the entire viewfinder. You can try different exposures and varied light sources – the window, an overhead lamp and so on.

When the pictures are developed, see which light souce and exposure gives you the sharpest and most detailed photograph. You can repeat the experiment with the finished work and keep both snaps for comparison.

Right: Snaps of a painting and its preparatory drawing taken inside and finally outside on a balcony, with as much sun as I could find.

60-Minute Projects

Tom Robb

1. Drawing a self-portrait

There are two things to aim for in painting portraits: to create a lively, mobile face with plenty of personality and eyes that seem as if they are really looking out of the frame and, not least, to paint a likeness of the sitter.

Sitting for a portrait almost always starts with a surprising amount of nervous tension as both sitter and painter come to terms with each other underneath the casual comments and social chit-chat.

For this reason, beginning the study of portraiture by drawing a self-portrait is an ideal project. All the little niceties can go by the board; there's no need to worry about the effect you are having (and about the quality of your finished portrait), you can concentrate on what you are actually painting. You know the face in the mirror and it makes a perfect model for your first attempts.

Three-quarter views are the best — facing straight into a mirror can be very disconcerting, but if you start too much on one side, you'll need to move your head too much when looking down and sideways at the paper. Find a chair, set it sideways at a comfortable angle in front of a mirror and work on a table easel. If you prefer to you can always stand, but do remember that you must be in a comfortable position; if it is vital for a model to be at ease, think how much more important it is now when you are both model and artist.

Start with loose outlines, keeping your wrist light, and block in simple shapes. You can use charcoal, red chalk (which makes a lovely warm portrait) or pastels. If it is the first time you have tried a self-portrait, then I suggest you use the red chalk. It concentrates the mind on shape and form, without your having to think about detailed colour matching (hair, for example, is quite difficult to get right, being such a mixture of tone and texture), while the sienna tones add enough warmth to keep the drawing from being too cold and impersonal.

Watch for the highlights, using a little white chalk where the light seems to fall; this will also help to give the head shape and depth. Side lighting can be a good strong feature, making it easy to see the shadows.

Shape the features by starting with lines, then smudging them to create whole areas of shadow and light. As you work, you'll find you are thinking less about your familiar self and more about the model in front of you; we all have two sides to our faces, with planes, bumps, creases and muscles running in slightly different directions. Make the most of this to capture that individual feature; check details like the space between the eyebrows, and from the earlobe to the jawline below; look at the shape of the mouth, the distance to the nose and chin, and the way the muscles in the neck hold up the head.

Below and right: Various stages in drawing a self-portrait, using first a few light strokes to set the portrait on the page, then roughing in the main tones; next an experiment in charcoal, looking straight ahead, then another charcoal drawing, more heavily shaded; finally a little more length added to the portrait.

If you find a whole head portrait impossible, go back to the beginning and make light, quick sketches of just the outline of your three-quarter face, with perhaps the eyes and eyebrows added, the line of hair brushed back, the highlight down the nose. Once you are comfortable with such half-sketches you can put them together another time with the same light touch, keeping your wrist loose and light.

2. Stretching, sizing and priming a canvas

The essential equipment for stretching and sizing a canvas is a stretcher with its wedges (see photograph), a set square (to make an absolutely rigid 90-degree angle), enough canvas to cover the stretcher plus 2 inches (5 cm) all around, either primed or unprimed, some upholstery tacks, a hammer and a pair of canvas pliers. The latter are sold in any art supply store; they are expensive but they last a lifetime.

When you buy the stretcher, check that all the wedges are there, then remove them and, by tapping gently with the hammer, make sure that all the joints are firmly in place.

Next check that the stretcher is square; all the corners should be right angles.

Cut out a piece of canvas, allowing for the extra 2 inches (5 cm), and lay it down on the table, primed or painting side down.

Put the stretcher down in the centre of the canvas front or right side down. The front of a stretcher is bevelled away from the canvas to avoid making ridges on the finished surface.

Fold the top edge of the canvas back over the stretcher and pin it down with one tack in the centre, and one on either side. (See illustration.) Now turn the frame around so the tacks are at the bottom.

The next bit is slightly awkward. You need to grasp the middle of the top of the canvas with the pliers, pull it over on to the stretcher and, holding the pliers steady to keep it taut, push in a tack on the edge just above the pliers, tapping it in with a hammer in your other hand. There is a fine line between keeping the canvas taut and pulling so hard that it is torn.

Now turn the frame 90 degrees again so that one untacked end is at the top and repeat, holding the pliers and making one tack in the middle. Repeat for the opposite end. The canvas is held taut on each side.

Moving back to the top, work outwards from the centre; hold the canvas taut with the pliers and tack down in place, roughly 1½ inches (38 mm) apart. Work around the frame as before.

Note: You must not put all the tacks in one side at once; moving around gradually stretches the canvas equally in all directions.

Tap the wedges in gently all around, fold the corners of the canvas neatly and put one tack in each corner to hold the fold down.

Look carefully to make sure the canvas is evenly stretched. If you have put the wedges in too hard, the frame might buckle or the canvas split.

Once an unprimed canvas is stretched it should be primed as soon as possible since the primer will tighten the canvas even more as it dries and shrinks.

1

2

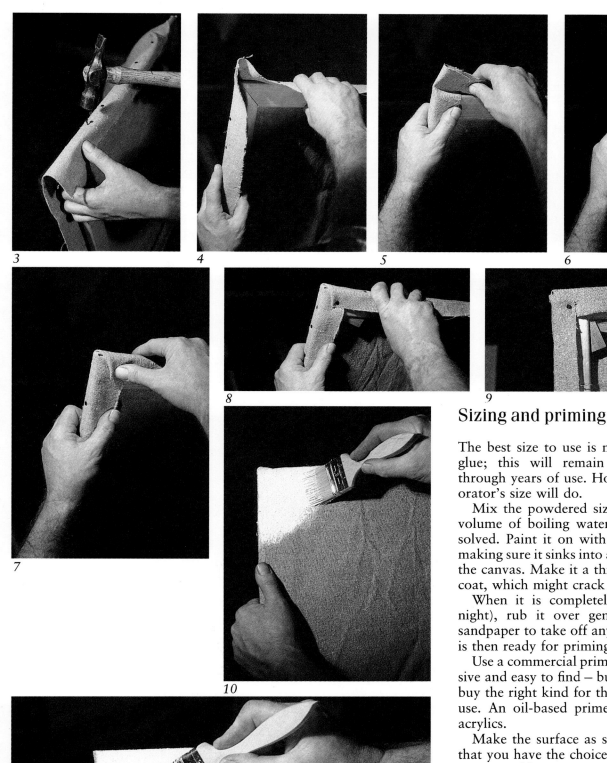

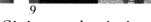

3

4

5

6

7

8

9

10

11

Sizing and priming

The best size to use is made from rabbitskin glue; this will remain pliable and supple through years of use. However, ordinary decorator's size will do.

Mix the powdered size with four times its volume of boiling water; stir until fully dissolved. Paint it on with a decorator's brush, making sure it sinks into all the irregularities of the canvas. Make it a thin rather than a thick coat, which might crack as it dries.

When it is completely dry (usually overnight), rub it over gently with a piece of sandpaper to take off any superfluous hairs. It is then ready for priming.

Use a commercial primer – they are inexpensive and easy to find – but make sure that you buy the right kind for the paint you intend to use. An oil-based primer is not suitable for acrylics.

Make the surface as smooth as possible so that you have the choice later of whether you want to add texture or not.

One or two fine coats are sufficient; allow the first to dry thoroughly.

Ideally, newly primed canvas should be left for some time before being used; old-fashioned text books used to say a year was soon enough to allow the canvas to become 'well seasoned'. This is probably unnecessary with modern primers, but a week or two is certainly recommended, especially in a humid climate.

Note: Don't be tempted to dry the primer in front of a fire or radiator – it will shrink badly and split.

3. Cutting a mount

The appearance of drawings and watercolours is always improved by their being mounted behind a card frame, which is called window mounting.

This helps to protect the edges, and it becomes very important when the painting is covered with glass. The mount creates a tiny air gap between the glass and the picture, thus preventing any friction on the surface and avoiding any damage if the glass changes temperature in varied conditions.

Ideally, you should use an acid-free card for the mount which actually touches the paper.

These do not come in a wide variety of colours, but you can always add another mount on top to create a double layer, giving extra protection as well as a pleasantly distinguished frame.

Mounting card varies in weight from thin box card to heavy mounting board. I don't like the very thin boards — they seem a waste of time except for simply mounting a large number of pictures to keep in a portfolio. On the other hand, very heavy board is difficult to cut, and if added to glass and a frame creates a weighty picture indeed!

Equipment

Mounting card, acid-free. White is a basic colour which is usually suitable for any picture, but if you have something special then you can choose from a number of pastel tones in creams and greys.

A one-metre stainless steel straight edge. This must be at least 2 inches (5 cm) wide, 1/8 inch (3 mm) thick, and bevelled on one edge — very expensive, true, but an investment for all time. Narrower steel rulers can be used, but they are much harder to work with and can be positively dangerous as they slip and slide

under pressure. Don't attempt to use a plastic ruler and a pen knife — apart from considerations of safety, the job will be badly finished.

A sturdy craft knife or a strong scalpel. A pencil, rubber and masking tape.

A cutting board. Use an old sheet of very thick card, a piece of smooth hardboard or a graphics cutting board — another worthwhile long-term investment, as they are made with a slight texture on top so the paper is held securely.

1

2

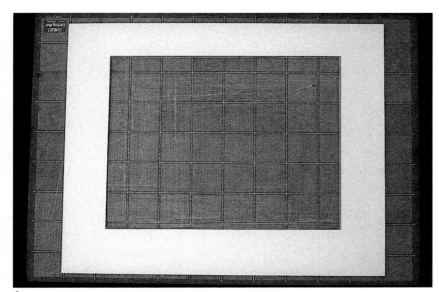

3

4

Measuring the mount

The prime measurement is at least 2 inches (5 cm) of mount around the top and sides of the area you wish to show, with an extra depth of around 2½ inches (63 mm) at the bottom. Measure the painting or drawing with it lying face up so you can make sure you are showing all the area you want, or hiding torn edges or a messy bit at the side which you would rather not exhibit. At the same time, the window must be smaller than the actual paper so that the drawing can be taped safely behind its frame.

Draw the outline of the window lightly on the card. If you are not quite sure of the measurements, make the window smaller; it is possible to cut away extra space later, but not possible to put it back!

Place the bevelled edge of the straight edge against the pencilled line. Cut cleanly, holding the knife resting on the edge so that it creates a bevelled edge on the mount. It is important to keep more pressure on the straight edge than on the knife, so that the former will not slip. A basic mistake is to press hard on the knife and use the ruler only as a guide, especially when it is too narrow. This is dangerous, as the knife will slip not only across the paper but sometimes on to the hand.

Cut almost to each corner, then take out the corners carefully with a few flicks of the knife to lift the inner piece away.

Check that the window shows the area of the painting that you want, then on the back measure the outside border and cut that against the straight edge (not the bevelled side).

Rub away any stray marks on the front and tape the painting in place with masking tape on the back, being careful to use enough to keep the picture safe even if it comes into contact with other paintings.

If you want to finish the mount off professionally before you tape the picture on, carefully lay a little gold leaf on to the bevelled edge.

Repeat exactly the same process for a double mount, cutting it large enough to create a window for the first mount as well as for the painting – usually ½ inch (13 mm) or so extra.

4. Making colour codes

Copy the chart given here in outline on to a similar-sized piece of sized and primed canvas or canvas board. There will be nine spaces for each colour.

You will need oil tubes of:
Lemon yellow
Cadmium yellow
Viridian green
Cobalt blue
Ultramarine
Prussian blue
Raw umber
Burnt umber
Lamp black

Put lemon yellow out in seven little dabs across the top of the colour code. Add a dab of each colour, except for cadmium yellow, to each separate yellow dab. Remember to clean the brush each time or the colours will mix.

Put cadmium yellow in seven little dabs on the line below, and go through the same process with the other colours, leaving out only the lemon yellow.

The result will give you fourteen basic greens, all mixtures of only two pigments. You can find an even greater range by mixing any two greens together, but the more colours you use the greyer and muddier the result. Many experimental colour mixes come adrift simply because the painter is trying just a little too hard to find something different. Always start with as few colours in a mixture as possible.

Once you begin experimenting with the various colours you mix for the code you may find one or two you want to make a note of for regular use, as there are relatively few modulations in green available already mixed. Even if you never use the colour codes for study or comparision it is a great help to know what mixtures will give you different greens quickly, especially if you are a landscape painter.

You can do the same with lilacs based on three blues (Prussian, ultramarine and cobalt) and with three reds (cadmium, alizarin crimson and Venetian red or Indian red). Oranges can be made up from three reds and lemon yellow, cadmium yellow and cadmium yellow deep.

Cadmium yellow	Cadmium yellow 3 / Yellow ochre 1	Cadmium yellow 2 / Yellow ochre 2	Cadmium yellow 1 / Yellow ochre 3	Yellow ochre
Cadmium yellow	Cadmium yellow 3 / Raw sienna 1	Cadmium yellow 2 / Raw sienna 2	Cadmium yellow 1 / Raw sienna 3	Raw sienna
Cadmium yellow	Cadmium yellow 3 / Light red 1	Cadmium yellow 2 / Light red 2	Cadmium yellow 1 / Light red 3	Light red
Cadmium yellow	Cadmium yellow 3 / Indian red 1	Cadmium yellow 2 / Indian red 2	Cadmium yellow 1 / Indian red 3	Indian red
Cadmium yellow	Cadmium yellow 3 / Cadmium red 1	Cadmium yellow 2 / Cadmium red 2	Cadmium yellow 1 / Cadmium red 3	Cadmium red
Cadmium yellow	Cadmium yellow 3 / Alizarin crimson 1	Cadmium yellow 2 / Alizarin crimson 2	Cadmium yellow 1 / Alizarin crimson 3	Alizarin crimson
Cadmium yellow	Cadmium yellow 3 / Raw umber 1	Cadmium yellow 2 / Raw umber 2	Cadmium yellow 1 / Raw umber 3	Raw umber
Cadmium yellow	Cadmium yellow 3 / Burnt umber 1	Cadmium yellow 2 / Burnt umber 2	Cadmium yellow 1 / Burnt umber 3	Burnt umber

5. A corner of a room

The space inside a room can be as wonderfully exciting and as worthy of exploration as the wildest landscape.

Most of us used to walk through a house as if the rooms were merely an empty area around our bodies, simply receptacles to hold chairs for sitting in, chests to keep clothes, etc. Decorators, home stylists and magazine articles have made us much more conscious of how full of colour and patterns a room can be, but they concentrate on the immediate appeal of the contents rather than the room as a place – the newly installed fitted wardrobe for example, not the spacial dimensions of ceiling to floor, skirting to ceiling rose. Indeed, the old-fashioned look of a dresser filled with a collection of 19th-century china is attractive enough to make most of us forget to look at the subtler proportions of wood and old glass, or the tiny variations in colour on the transfer printing on the china, the faded chintzes or the modern radio.

Use an hour to really look at a room in your house as if you had arrived from a different planet. Outdoors, the horizon can be miles and miles away; here it is only a few feet.

First, try to ignore the personal meaning of the objects; look for the spiky outline of a chair, the lumpy outline of a sofa, the pattern of shelves, the roundness of handles.

Play around with one piece of furniture, putting things on top, pulling out drawers or covering the whole thing with a white sheet. Now isolate a corner, put a chair or a table by the wall and add a few cushions, a lamp and another chair or stool in front to make a group.

In the next project there will be more complex perspective drawings which help to create three-dimensional areas.

Right: A sketch which began with a wonderful planted bowl, expanding gradually to include its setting (across, top) of the corner where it had been placed on a table next to a chair. You may often need to begin with a detail like the bowl in order to get a feeling for its shape and texture, but don't forget to move back to include the chair.

6. Sketching people in the park

This is a series of quick sketches in a small notebook which you should make as unobtrusively as possible (it makes people self-conscious if they see they are being used as models). Work with pencils, coloured pencils or felt pens. Practise using your eyes carefully so that an occasional casual glance is enough to check your model; it will keep everyone comfortable and happy, and you'll be able to work for quite long periods.

You may find yourself giving drawing lessons to an inquisitive child, but that can be quite fun, too, and the promise of a sketch of themselves or their teddy bear is usually enough for at least 30 seconds' peace.

Practise with some of those memory tests that children have – how many items on a table you can remember after just a quick glance, for example. Train yourself with a tray of objects prepared by a friend, giving yourself gradually lessening amounts of time to look and remember. As you begin to improve, make the test more appropriate for your purpose by also including people and having to remember different colours, clothes, faces, hairstyles, and so on.

7. Perspective

There are so many obscure diagrams in most 'Perspective and How to Use It' studies that it is a wonder most new artists don't give up at once and turn gratefully back to painting just what they see.

As long as we remember that it is simply an optical illusion, a mathematical tool by which to create a three-dimensional world on the two-dimensional flat canvas, perspective comes into its own. It can be very useful in particular kinds of projects: architectural drawings, for example; cityscapes where the buildings must look in line with each other and have receding doors and windows; and paintings that contain a great deal of surface decoration on angles and corners, or that feature objects that need to look completely solid.

The very earliest Egyptian paintings were drawn with no attempt at creating the reality of three dimensions; the flat shapes of the figures were set one behind the other to create the armies of people disappearing into the distance, or were just made larger and smaller to indicate how far away they were from the viewer.

By the time Greek and Roman art was flourishing, the flat Egyptian figures had given way to paintings using shadows and colours to create depth. This is the simplest form of perspective, and in many ways the most natural. It is called 'aerial', because the effects upon which it depends are created in the air by the atmosphere and the changes in weather. Distant mountains become grey and blurred on the horizon, trees cast their shadows, grasses loom large in the foreground. If an artist is sufficiently observant, recording these changes in both colour and tone will be enough to make an entirely convincing three-dimensional painting.

However, by the time of the Renaissance, architects and artists had worked out a formal system of linear perspective which would allow them to make accurate drawings on a grand scale featuring the classical draperies, columns, niches and patterned marble floors that they adored.

In its essence this is the same system we use today, although the great period of neo-realism seems to be over and many artists are becoming more selective and taking only those ideas about perspective which they feel enhance their own personal style. Some, indeed, follow the method used so magnificently by Cézanne and Picasso of deliberately altering the perspective to create an effect.

However, any distortion of reality should ideally come from deliberate use, not ignorance. Learning the basics of perspective theory is still important even if you never use it in your paintings.

Learning to use linear perspective

In linear perspective any flat, two-dimensional surface such as a sheet of glass is called a plane. All perspective is based on the eye level of an imaginary observer.

He stands on the flat ground plane. Looking straight ahead, think of the observer as holding an imaginary sheet of glass vertically in front of the object; this is the picture plane.

Linear perspective is simply an imaginary way of copying the receding lines you see through the glass on to the glass itself, and then transferring them to the real canvas and so re-creating the view in the painting.

If the objects in the picture are correctly drawn, then if you extend any parallel lines they should meet on the horizon, at what is called the vanishing point. If not, then you haven't drawn them properly. All the parallel lines in one picture will meet at the same vanishing point on the horizon. Look at the kitchen floor; if its black and white tiles, laid down with parallel grouting, stretched to the horizon then their images would all recede to one vanishing point. All objects drawn from the same point of view, or eye level, should have parallel lines that meet at the same level on the horizon, although at different places.

When an object has a flat side towards you, its two parallel sides meet at one vanishing point; see the railway in the diagram. If it has a corner towards you there will be two vanishing points, and if the object is tilted up or down it will give you three vanishing points. This is called one-point, two-point and three-point perspective.

Perspective gives you a useful check when you are drawing two or more buildings, areas of paving, ornamentation, and so on. Very often these are quite difficult to draw precisely and they many end up looking awkwardly placed; making an outline copy and extending their parallel lines will show immediately if you have drawn them from the same point of view.

Most artists rely on their own observation to get proportions and lines correctly placed, but a knowledge of formal perspective can help, especially if the picture involves architecture. However, one word of warning; it is, after all, an artificial technique, and it should never replace the human eye. There is nothing more lifeless and boring than a completely accurate, mathematically produced drawing that could have been safely left to a computer.

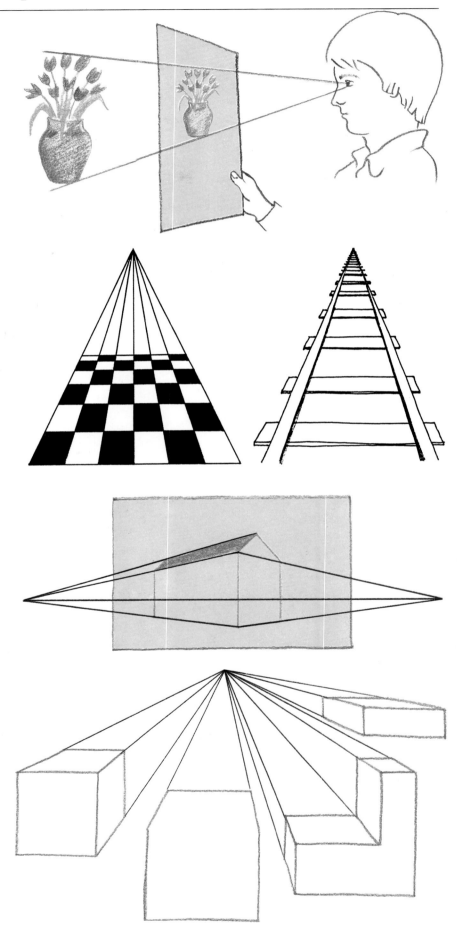

Renaissance perspective studies

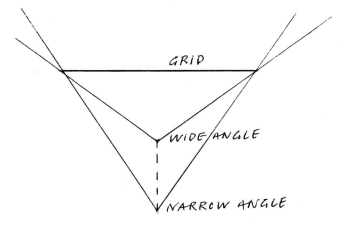

By the end of the 17th century perspective had already become a scientific system. Some artists who were desperate to achieve absolute perfection worked from a grid, carefully built with strings on a wooden frame, and large enough to set up at the end of their drawing table. A wooden support with a viewing hole could be moved nearer or further away from the grid, changing the area which the artist was painting from a narrow cone to a wide angle.

The result was a carefully constructed drawing which could then be taken back to the studio and turned into a similarly precise painting.

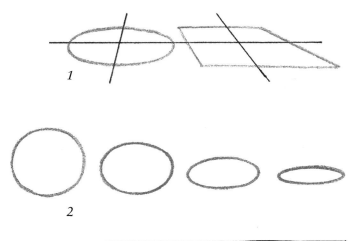

1. Here is a simple outline drawing of a circle and square, both tilted to show how they would look laid on a flat plane. Imagine, perhaps, that the circle is a round plate, the square a table napkin.

Practise drawing shapes in various positions; upright in front of you, then gradually tilted down and up, and from side to side.

2. In this exercise, the circle, seen face on, is gradually tilted back in four stages until it becomes an ellipse, lying on a horizontal surface. The plate, in other words, upright on a stand, is gradually laid back on to the table.

3. Here is an example of how illusion works for the artist, and how actual measurements need to be adjusted so that the result appears to be correct.

This is called the corridor effect. Look at the nearest and middle bars; because the lines of perspective show a corridor leading away from us, the nearest bar looks as if it is much smaller than the bar halfway down the corridor. This is because the first two bars are seen in relation to the surrounding corridor; in fact, they are exactly the same size. The third bar has been adjusted in height and width so that it runs between the same two parallel lines as the first bar, and if you look only at the first and third bars they appear to be a natural progression.

8. Variations on watercolour washes

Applying washes is the basic technique of almost all watercolour painting – in fact, the same method is also the basis of ink drawings with added wash, and even of some oil and acrylic paintings where the pigment is laid on the canvas in broad washes.

The art of watercolour washes is the first technique to be learned, but there are many variations which should be explored. Multi-coloured washes build up tone to make subtle and evocative landscapes or seascapes with no more than a few wide swathes of the brush. For the best effect, every layer must be bone dry before you add the next.

Washing out creates highlights without having to manoeuvre the washes around the shapes you want to leave white. You'll need to use good-quality paper; cheap cartridge paper will be roughed up when you take away the pigment, leaving a nasty patch on your picture.

Wash in a light blue sky and let it dry completely. Take a perfectly clean brush, loaded with clear water, and 'paint' the area where you want to create white clouds. The water will become slightly tinted on the paper; blot it with a rag, or a damp sponge, without rubbing. Repeat until the area is absolutely clean of any colour. This gives a sharp edge to the patch of white; for a smudgier effect use a bit of clean, damp sponge.

Working on wet washes is even more subtle, achieving remarkable effects with just a splash of colour here and there.

The principle is exactly the opposite; the paper is dampened down and the brush, loaded with pigment, is used again and again without waiting for the first layer to dry. Sometimes the paper can be tilted up or down to control the run-off and encourage the appearance of shadowy, blurry areas.

On this page, examples of washing out and working wet on wet; opposite, the effects of layering, and how to create subtle transparent colours with a variety of washes.

9. A still life

Go back to the still-life group you put together in 30 minutes. Look at it critically, deciding if you think it will work for you, and make changes if you are not pleased with the general effect. There is no point in spending time on a painting you are not interested in doing – the feeling of uncertainty will communicate itself to your work.

Place a chair for yourself or set up a light easel to the most interesting side of the group. As a change from the earlier projects try using watercolour, which is a good medium for putting the emphasis on tone and colour. You can also use charcoal or ink wash if you prefer.

Think about the light. Natural light can be used in a variety of ways, especially if your room has an outside door. Prop the door open and see if you like the effect; try pushing the curtains aside to increase the light from the windows. As this project will only be for an hour the natural light won't change very much, which can be quite useful.

Experiment with a table lamp, but avoid using a central ceiling light unless you can make a mask of muslin or sheeting material, as suggested on page 50; it usually looks too bland and too widespread to be effective.

Now sit down and look for a moment, deciding exactly what you want to include, and where the drawing will stop and start.

Using thin sticks of fine willow charcoal, begin by doing a very light outline drawing, indicating where the main objects are with a few light touches. Remember to use as much of the paper as possible.

Look again at the group and decide which is the darkest object. In this case it is the background of the bookcase, especially behind the rose, and this ensures that the background is dominant – as it was in that earlier composition (page 41), albeit in an entirely different way. The case and the dividing line of the books were therefore painted first, as they constitute the deepest tone.

Which object is lightest in tone? The plate, the chair, the top of the cheese? These are going to be left white. Then comes the tone that is almost the darkest, then almost the lightest, until all the objects are on the page.

Look for modulations. The curved surface of the fruit changes from dark to light, the cups and plates less so. The top rim of the chair shadows the rails underneath. The rose relies entirely on the dark and light splashes of colour to make it sing out, with just the briefest reflection in the glass.

Avoid drawing any heavy black lines around the objects; colour and shadow will make the drawing work, not outline. The objects will find their own place in space, and the shadows will describe them without the need to add that artificial line.

The final touches are to highlight any contrast by making a dark tone darker, a light tone whiter.

Wash your hands then go around the picture with a rubber, getting rid of any light pencil marks that still show.

If you have used charcoal, spray with an aerosol fixative, carefully following the instructions on the can. If you spray too close the fixative will run, too far away and it will cover everything else but the picture and be totally ineffective.

Pin the picture on the wall where you can see it often, not only deliberately but when you pass by and catch it from a different angle. Everything you do, every project and every sketch, can help you learn to judge your own work intelligently and objectively, separating the successful pictures from the good tries which haven't quite worked and from the frankly awful. If you feel like despairing, don't. Even after a lifetime of professional achievement, any artist will have quite a large number of works which fall into that last category. They are proof of the fact that we all have to go on learning, all the time.

Below: A detail from a wonderful painting by Bonnard. Note that the shadows are not painted black or brown in the usual way, but are a reflection of Bonnard's fascination with glowing colour – the chairback shadow is a purply blue.

Across: A simple way to try your hand at a still life, looking for tones and colour, and unusual colour in the shadows.

Two-Hour Projects

1. Painting a landscape outdoors
2. Grinding your own oil paint
3. Painting an interior
4. Tinted and textured papers
5. Palettes and their history
6. Aerial perspective
7. Using a palette knife
8. Making your own pastels
9. Sketching a street scene
10. Lighting a model

1. Painting a landscape outdoors

Before setting out to paint you need a few minutes to get equipment ready. For working quickly out of doors watercolour is the most varied and flexible medium, quick to put on and to dry. You can use acrylic thinned with water, but the colour range is not as good and there is no real advantage unless you want to do quick oil-like sketches without waiting for oil pigments to dry.

Equipment

This is a good mix of colours to begin with:
Cadmium yellow
Yellow ochre
Cadmium red
Raw sienna
Burnt umber
Viridian
Ultramarine
Ivory black
A largish sable brush and a smaller one; perhaps a number 4 and number 8
A pad of watercolour paper; these are ready for use. However, if you want to paint on a larger scale, take one or two pieces of heavy watercolour paper, stretched and on their boards, with a small sketchbook for preliminary ideas and composition
A small plastic bottle of water with a tight cap. Just ½ pt (250 ml) of water is more than enough for two or three pictures, leaving plenty for washing out the brushes as well. However, take more than you need at first until you get accustomed to your own methods of working
Paint, brushes and water can go into a bag, with some white paper tissues or a rag; the smaller sketchbooks should fit in as well
You can be as frugal as you like with equipment; two brushes will give you plenty of variation in laying washes and in using the points for fine detail. In fact, many painters (including myself) who might be tempted to give a long list of watercolour brushes to their students actually use only one for their own sketching trips!

Looking for a view

I always prefer to begin landscapes outdoors, even if I finish later in the studio. However, 'outdoors' can mean the end of the garden or a famous beauty spot miles away.

When you work on ideas from different viewpoints, remember that your eyes have a very wide peripheral vision and it would make an impossibly complicated picture if you tried to paint everything you actually see.

The artist's eye is like a searchlight, looking for a small circle or square within the open frame of nature. There should be one strong image to focus on – a particular angle, a bed of flowers or a fountain, a curving path or a massive tree, an attractive barn or church.

I chose a place looking across a meadow. There were houses and a road just out of the picture on the left, and a rather large and ugly farm on the right. However, just within the encompassing trees, there was the church, a flock of sheep, and a few rounded groups of trees to provide balance.

Now find somewhere to sit – a large stone, a bench, or a bit of a wall. You'll want to think about what you plan to paint, because every painting makes some sort of statement. Be prepared to spend a good few minutes deciding why you chose that spot, and what in particular you want to say about it. Perhaps making a number of small sketches will help you to decide on the approach.

Here are a few ways the same view can be tackled by the artist:

1. As a collection of things: a church, a group of trees, a sheep. Each object can be painted separately, standing in its place. This is a documentary approach.

2. As colours and shapes, ignoring the objects as such; an abstract of reality, based on pattern and design.

3. With an emotional response, capturing the atmosphere of the place which you want to record; the wind is blowing, so the trees become tormented and bent over, the sky lowering and gloomy – or perhaps you see just the opposite; an image of tranquillity and peace, the sheltering trees, the quiet continuity of the landscape.

Make a habit of thinking through each attempt at a painting in this way.

You can try out your ideas with quick sketches before you choose which of the approaches you want to use.

Then start painting on a larger scale, laying in the main washes, working at first all over the picture so that it develops evenly. Concentrate on the particular approach you have chosen.

In the second hour, fill in the details. If you are working on a scene like this one, wash out the white patches for the sheep, add touches to the roof of the church, drop in a few colours for flowers and perhaps the skirt of a passing walker or a bit of curtain blowing in the breeze far away in the rectory.

Work only for the two hours; all of these projects are designed to give you the discipline of working to a set time. When you know you have to finish at a certain point it provides an impetus which prevents you from getting bogged down on some infuriating detail.

If you are really intrigued with the scene work there again, deliberately using a different approach, perhaps one which you don't really enjoy at first. Comparing the two paintings can be fascinating, and you might find that you begin to see things in a different way.

If you find you enjoy sketching outdoors, make yourself a carrying case (see page 148).

Right: You needn't go very far to find a pleasant view to paint. Here's a small landscape of sorts made at the bottom of my garden one day when I couldn't travel as I had planned. I used the same approach of trying to think through the subject, deciding that in this case I was most interested in the individual shapes and abstract forms.

In fact I almost left the little sketch at the second stage, with only the three main tones in place, but the fun of the fence bars and the extra fluffiness of the trees won the day!

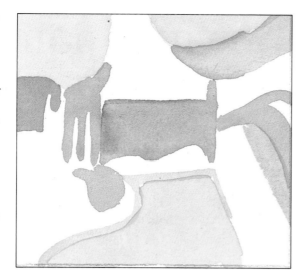

2. Grinding your own oil paint

Today there are so many commercial paint manufacturers that it is unusual to find someone grinding their own, as all traditional artists did until well into this century. However, there are still a few good reasons for learning this centuries-old technique:

★ Economy; you can usually make quite a saving by doing the hard work yourself, and there are many containers on the market in which to keep the finished pigments.

★ As you develop an individual style, your work may perhaps be better suited to either a dryer or more liquid paint, a grittier or a finer texture.

★ A liking for special colours which you can grind for yourself but which are not available ready-made.

★ Most important, grinding your own colours at least once will add enormously to your understanding of pigment, colour, mixing and so on.

Equipment

Powder colour (various pigments are available from any good art store).
There are three basic kinds of pigment; metal oxides, earth colours, and artificial dye colours, which need special treatment.

Cold-pressed linseed oil and/or poppy oil
White Beeswax
Glass muller, around 2½–3 inches (63–76 mm) wide
Slab of white marble, around 18 inches (45 cm) square, or a similar piece of very thick plain glass, with a piece of paper underneath so you can see the changes in colour as the pigment becomes paint
Palette knife or flexible spatula for mixing
Small polythene self-sealing bags
Small jars and empty oil tubes ready for filling
Bowl for the initial mixing
Gauze face mask and a pair of rubber gloves
Note: Some pigments can be toxic if inhaled or handled too much. Always wear a gauze face mask and rubber gloves while you are grinding and measuring any powders.

Mix a small quantity of powder colour and add enough linseed oil to make a stiff paste. Some light colours may be turned slightly yellow by the linseed oil, so substitute poppy oil for these. It takes longer to dry once the paint is on the canvas, but it does keep whites and pale colours bright.

Although most artists grind only the basic colours, mixing what they want in the way of compound colours on the palette, if you use a great deal of a particular mixture you will find it much more convenient to create it directly from the powdered colour. However, you will have to keep careful notes of quantities and proportions so that you get the same colour each time.

Make sure the pigment is well mixed into the oil so that it is distributed equally.

Now, with a small amount of the paste on the marble slab, begin grinding with the muller, and you will see that the paste gradually becomes a liquid.

Add a few small bits of beeswax to the mixture to stabilize it – no more than 2 per cent by weight of the whole.

Colours can be finely or coarsely ground; if the pigment still feels gritty it is probably too coarse for everyday use, although there are some painters who find that extra texture is one of the best reasons for grinding their own paint in the first place!

As the liquid forms, some colours will need more oil and therefore a longer grinding time; the earth colours, viridian and cobalt blue, and lamp black, for example, will soak up a great

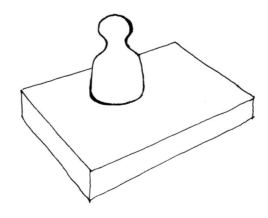

Left: A muller, similar to a pestle but flatter. Across: An array of pigments and tubes of paint.

deal of oil, up to ten times as much as usual, while venetian red and zinc white absorb very little.

When the paint has reached an ideal consistency for your work pack it carefully into polythene bags, making sure you leave no air spaces to cause lumps. If you are using jars you will need to ensure they are packed right to the top and covered with a polythene circle held down tightly with a rubber band, rather as if you were making jam.

You can also buy empty metal tubes which are filled from the bottom, folded over and used in the ordinary way. You can push the paint in with a thin palette knife, but because you can't see what you are doing you are more likely to get air bubbles, which form a skin and block the nozzle.

3. Painting an interior

The subject of interiors offers a whole new dimension to painting. With still lifes and individual objects, even with portraits, your vision is narrowed to what is more or less directly in front of your eyes. However, step back to take in a room and the vocabulary of painting is doubled. Look through a doorway into another space, and you are part of that outside world.

You may think of your home as simply a

background to the people who live there, or as a place for family occasions – both good and bad. However, an empty room can provide a more powerful expression of personality than any historical essay; think of the cool, clear light of a Dutch interior, the wildly gyrating colours of Van Gogh's empty chair, the glowing Mediterranean afternoon of a Bonnard bedroom.

Add a living figure, animal or human, and however small the figure is the scene becomes a stage set. It can tell a story – the empty chair and a waiting dog stretched by the fireplace, or the dining room set for an important party, the anxious hostess lighting the candles – or it can develop its own personality, the pattern and decoration blending with the figure to make a richer painting.

Even on a small domestic scale, you can succeed in capturing the individual quality of a place, which is such a delight to recognize – so find a room which you enjoy visiting, or any place you find comfortable and warm (or cold and forbidding!).

Look at it now through the eyes of a painter. Look for colour, shape, dimension and space, relationships between the contents and the architecture, the way the room makes you feel, and for the clues it gives to the visitor seeing it for the first time about the people who live or work there.

The first decision should be, as always, on the approach you are going to take. With a richly decorated room there is a chance to develop a precise interest in detail – the fold of a curtain, the pattern at the edge of the carpet. However, with only two hours to work, I would suggest a freer technique which concentrates on atmosphere.

Standing beside your easel, look for the ways the light is coming in; from the window, a lamp, or an open door. Where are the highlights, and where is the deeper shadow? Try not to paint any objects at all, but the light which touches them – make suggestions of objects, indications of colour, shadows, shades and tones, curls of outlines, texture of walls.

Work all over the paper, flicking in odd touches of colour here and there, stepping back often to see the painting as if you were coming into the room for the first time.

The most important single aspect of any enclosed space is the light; no matter what the design or colour, if there is nothing but gloom and darkness there will be only misery in view, while the poorest room, flooded with warm lamp- or sunlight, can be surprisingly cheerful. Here I was lucky enough to find a room so full of warm reds and golds that it cried out for the soft glow of pastels, and there were so many lovely decorative patterns that I was quite happy to lose my model to the demands of the telephone while I worked around the empty chair. Remember to use a little artistic licence for large areas like the foreground – I keyed up the rather drab beige carpet to a soft apricot, and for a finished painting I might well have added another table or chairback to balance the empty space. This is not a portrait, so there is no need to try for a likeness; in fact, the figure is simply another design in the overall pattern of the room.

4. Tinted and textured papers

Paper is the fundamental material for almost all watercolour and sketching artists. Very few new students have any idea how many different kinds of paper there are, and how the choice of paper, its quality, material, manufacturing and colour, can add to or detract from the finished work.

The three main grades of paper surface are:
Rough; the thickest paper with the greatest amount of tooth; best for free, impressionistic work
Not, sometimes called **Cold press** (CP); the medium-rough surface for the average watercolour or pastel
Hot press (HP); the smoothest surface, best for fine ink and brushwork or detailed drawings.

These categories can refer to coloured papers, too; when there is a stronger tint such as beige, grey or blue the variations on the surface show up even more than they do in white.

Few of the hand-made papers with 100 per cent rag content are made in deep tints, although some come in lovely subtle tones of sand, grey, creams, greens, and a natural white with no optical brighteners.

If you are interested in discovering how to manipulate a variety of atmospheric effects, using coloured paper can make a great deal of sense, cutting out one stage in preparation work – instead of having to lay background washes, you can start immediately on the painting.

To see how the coloured papers will change your paints, buy a sheet of each colour you want to try and cut a strip off every one, mounting them on plain board. Using a clean brush each time, paint right across your set of papers with blues, greens, yellows, reds, etc. The more colours you use, the better your 'sampler' will be. Pin it up on the wall near your easel and it will be the perfect reference when you work.

Right, three versions of watercolour sketches on tinted paper; see how effective it can be to let the paper show through and act as part of the painting itself.

Pastel papers

Ingres is the traditional pastel paper, although it can be used with watercolours and crayons. It has a definite grain of woven lines, which an experienced artist will use as part of the picture. Because of the pattern it is more difficult to blend colours on the paper, so you will need to buy or make additional sticks if you want subtle shades. Ingres paper comes in at least 15 shades from black (really a dark grey) through browns, bronzes, blues, greens, pinks, etc.

The attraction here is the wide variety of effects you can achieve even when you use the same chalks and watercolours. The following spread has a range of different colours and surfaces; starting on the left, there is a smooth-surfaced pink, changing to a rougher pink with a watermark on the edge, to an Ingres pink, and going on through the Caslon colours to a very coarse-grained hand-made olive green paper. Look at the variation in the pastels and watercolours as they are pulled across, especially when they move over the watermark.

Notice how the watercolour spreads on the smooth papers and shows up the grain on the Caslon papers, especially on the deep yellow. This may give you some ideas for playing around with different subjects; think of the dark blue background for a bowl of richly coloured fruit and one brilliant lemon, a dark sienna drawing on the grey paper, a watercolour of autumn fields on the darkest gold.

There are other papers which are only suitable for pastels and have unusual surface texture:
Velvet or **Velour** paper; the almost-furry surface gives soft, blurry effects and is quite unsuitable for any kind of detail or crisp edges.
Sand-grain paper; as its name suggests, it is covered with a fine-grain, rough surface, used sometimes by woodworkers for final finishes. Blending the colours is very easy, but the pastel sticks are used up at a great rate. The basic colour is a soft beige, but it is sometimes made in grey.

Overleaf: A variety of papers in different colours and textures, showing how they react to the same pastels and watercolour pigments. Look especially at how the watermark shows up when the paint is thin, or when pastels are used, while it is completely obliterated by the heavier pigments or the busier patterns.

5. Palettes and their history

A traditional palette made of varnished wood is a lovely object to own; it is light, strong, and easily cut into any idiosyncratic shape. The artists' colourmen of the 18th and 19th centuries would make palettes to order, fitting them to the hand and arm of an individual painter so that there was perfect harmony in size, use and appearance.

There was always a choice of wood, too; mahogany was a favourite because it was tough, strong and light, but oak, walnut and later rosewood all had their adherents. The only requirement was that it should not warp – elm was never used for that reason. All the woods were polished or varnished so that the oil pigments would rest on the top without being absorbed. Some secret techniques involved soaking the wood in oil, others in coating it with gum or shellac and chalk.

Ladies would have smaller palettes, so that they didn't hamper the artist from working on tiny details. In contrast, the painters of the grand historical paintings often ordered a grand palette to match their ambitions.

In the Royal Academy in London, along with Sir Joshua Reynolds' own palette, there are three or four others, one cut unusually high, presumably to accommodate a short-armed painter. Small, square palettes are still especially made to fit inside the lids of painting boxes for working out of doors, but the thumbhole is seldom in exactly the right place to provide good balance.

The palette today

The usual size is about 18 inches (45 cm) long by 12 inches (30 cm) at its widest point. The body of the palette is made from chamfered or layered wood so that the side away from your thumb is light enough to balance beautifully on the arm without feeling heavy. Another way of making the palette balance is to add small lead weights at one end, but this obviously adds to the overall weight.

Other materials such as plastic and aluminium can be used when convenient; the only prerequisites are that the palette should be comfortable to hold, non-absorbent, easily cleaned and not too heavy.

A white palette is unusual, although originally small palettes were made of ivory and porcelain; this is a good idea for someone just beginning to paint, as the colours show up very clearly and the mixing of them is not affected by the darkness of more traditional materials.

The classic kidney shape is still the best, I feel, as it fits naturally to the body, the hand, and the sweep of the brush as you work. There are even right-handed palettes for left-handed painters.

The pads of throw-away paper palettes, preformed with a thumbhole, are useful in an emergency; after use the top sheet is simply pulled off and thrown away. However, a brand-new pad is quite heavy, a single sheet is too light, and in general I find the surface unpleasant and cardboardy — and very expensive. However, there is no doubt that on a long painting trip these pads really come into their own for convenience and ease of disposal.

Glimpsed by the camera; Cézanne and Matisse both used small square palettes out of doors, and traditional rounded ones at home.

Making a traditional palette

Equipment

A piece of card, 18 × 12 inches
(45 × 30 cm), to make a template of
the shape
A piece of mahogany 18 × 12 inches
(45 × 30 cm), ⅜ inch (9 mm) thick
A saw (either a jig, fret or pad saw)
A plane, knife and gouge
Fine sandpaper
Varnish or shellac polish

Cut the template out of the card and hold it to see that the thumb is in the right place; you must be able to hold brushes comfortably in the slot (called the mouth of the palette). The length should fit conveniently into the curve of your elbow.

Cut the shape out of the wood. You will have to feather it from the wide 'cheek', starting with ⅜ inch (9 mm) and feathering out to ⅛ inch (3 mm) at the edge of the blade at the other end.

Next cut the thumbhole with the knife and gouge, making sure it is at a slant so that the thumb can turn inwards.

Finish off all the cut edges with sandpaper and varnish at least twice, one side at a time so that it remains perfectly flat.

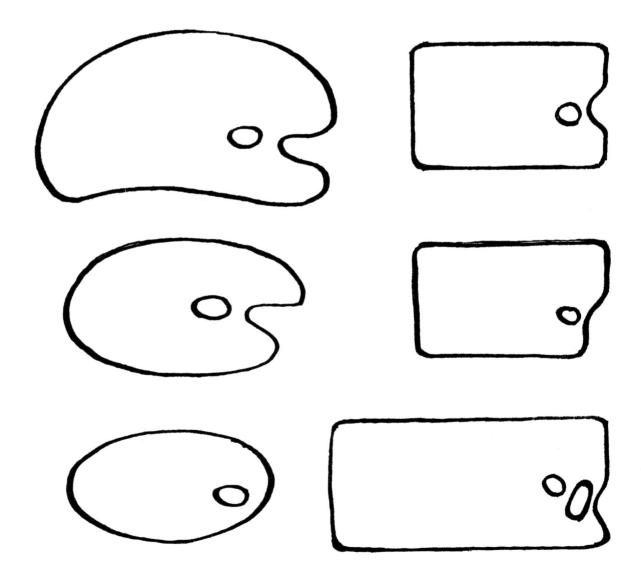

6. Aerial perspective

Linear perspective is a fairly complex idea about using sight lines to impose an image of three-dimensional objects on the flat plane of the picture. To use the theory of linear perspective you need to understand and manipulate certain rules and measurements (see p. 72).

However, there is another way of using perspective which is based on simple observation; the size of objects diminishes as they move further away from you, and colours and outlines change. An acutely observant painter, with no knowledge of the formal rules and requirements of linear perspective, can thus still record a scene with great accuracy.

If you have a landscape in front of you, look from the foreground to the horizon. Even the brightest colours will gradually fade to a much lighter, cooler shade. Great bushes of yellow and red flowers in warm, vibrant tones will fade to a cooler tone of beige; rich brown peatland will fade to a dusky ochre colour, and deep blues and purples become smoky blues and hazy violets.

Another change takes place, too; patterns and contrast fade, so that the colours of a red and yellow pole seen crisp and clear in the foreground will become indistinct as it merges into the background.

Outlines become blurred and detail almost disappears. Imagine a stage, with curtains at 5 ft (1.5 m) intervals intended to show a much greater depth than the reality; each set of curtains furthest from the front will become more and more blurred, less and less clearly patterned, and no matter what the front colouring, the last curtain will be some tone of grey. Using this simple idea, a stage 20 ft (6 m) deep can appear to be at least 100 ft (30 m) deep.

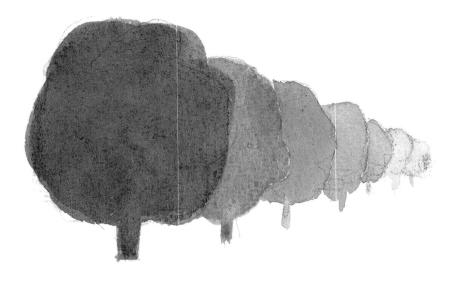

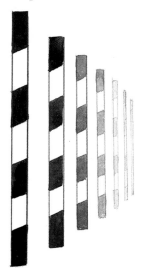

7. Using a palette knife

The traditional way of applying paint is with a brush, but in fact there are many other methods; you can use anything that seems useful, including your fingers.

However, one of the most popular tools is a knife, often called a palette knife. Technically speaking, the slightly longer, straight-edged palette knife is used to clean the palette, or to mix colour on it; applying paint to the canvas is supposed to be done with a painting knife, with a smaller head and, often, a triangular shape. In practical use these have become almost indistinguishable, and many artists will use whichever comes to hand first.

Why use a knife at all? The main advantage is the ability to cover a large area quickly and smoothly with oil or acrylic paint. The effect is very much like laying a watercolour wash – an even surface without brushmarks.

An additional layer can be added afterwards of chunky rectangles, marbling or watery patterns that are almost impossible to achieve with a brush.

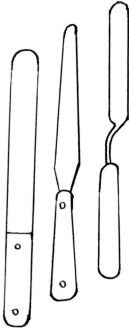

Another great advantage of painting with a knife is the ability to put on or remove small or large chunks of paint using the point. A typical use of the knife is shown here on the flower study. The petals are just flicks of pigment; the effect is instant and unique to the knife.

If you want to make scratches in the paint like graffito patterns in pottery, the edge of the knife will cut through the layers right down to the white canvas, which is impossible to achieve with a brush.

Of course, you can also build up areas to make a thick impasto wherever it is wanted. Unlike a brush, whose hairs hold paint as a kind of mini-supply system, the knife is clean and all the pigment is transferred to the place you want.

How to use the knife

Painting knives come in a wide variety of shapes and sizes; it is a matter of experience as to which suits your own needs. I have quite a few – some old and flexible carbon steel knives for delicate work, and some wider and heavier modern, stainless steel ones for laying large areas of paint. Pointed tips are useful for precise work, such as removing little flecks of paint. Round-ended knives are best for spreading.

The blade of any knife must be absolutely clean. The slightest blemish may start an attack of rust; an encrustation of old paint will make it impossible to create the sharp, clean edges which add so much to the effect.

Although knives may seem sturdier than a brush, they can in fact be damaged very easily, the edges becoming nicked or distorted. Clean them carefully after every use and store them handle down in a jar.

You must also be careful that the blades are not twisted, or working cleanly on the canvas will require so much distortion of your hand that you will get tired in a few minutes.

There are some very fine painting knives which are as flexible as paper, and these can be held and used as you would a brush. Hold anything larger rather as if you were using a garden trowel, with your thumb uppermost.

When you want to build paint into a really thick layer, you need to mix the pigment with warmed beeswax or paraffin wax on your palette to give it substance; it then won't crack or run off the canvas, no matter how much you put on. If you want really large amounts of impasto you can use a fine plaster, or plaster of Paris, but this can set very hard and may be more difficult to change or remove.

8. Making your own pastels

Making pictures with fine-ground pigment is one of the earliest forms of colouring. Throughout the history of art most coloured pastels were made in the studio by apprentices until commercial manufacture began in the 18th century.

Although there is a very wide range of pastels available today, making your own has two clear advantages: you can choose the size of the sticks, and the particular mixture and consistency you prefer. Of course, it also helps to teach you a great deal about the use of tools and the techniques suitable for each drawing surface.

Equipment

Powdered pigment (readily available from most good artists' suppliers)
Gum tragacanth in powdered form
Powdered chalk (calcium carbonate or whiting) – the amount will depend on the shade you are making (see Note 2))
A small glass of alcohol – vodka or gin for preference
Two or three china cups or bowls, depending on how many sticks you are making of each colour.
A sheet or two of greaseproof paper to cover the table

Note 1: You can substitute gum arabic for the gum tragacanth, but you will have to add a little plain flour or caster sugar to the mixture.

Put the pigment and chalk in a cup, pour in half the alcohol and mix well. This stops the pigment from becoming greasy and unable to mix with the gum solution.

Put the gum into one of the bowls and pour on enough hot water to make a saturated solution (roughly half a cup of gum to a cup of hot water).

Now add the gum solution to the pigment and stir in thoroughly. The texture will be like putty.

Wet your hands to keep the putty from sticking to them, form it into small blobs about the size of a cake of soap and leave until the texture becomes slightly stiff as the gum starts to set.

You will be able to roll the cakes into any shape you want – large sticks or blocks for drawing lovely big lines, or thin sticks for small details. Neither of these is available commercially.

Note 2: The proportion of chalk to pigment is about half and half, but if you want particularly dark pastels use less chalk and for very pale ones use much more. A pure white pastel can be made from half chalk and half titanium white pigment.

Earth colour pigments are excellent for making pastels and, for lighter shades, titanium white blends with other colours more easily than chalk.

Warning note

Some pigments are actively dangerous, especially in powdered form. All the chrome colours are particularly toxic, and must be handled with great care. Check with the supplier.

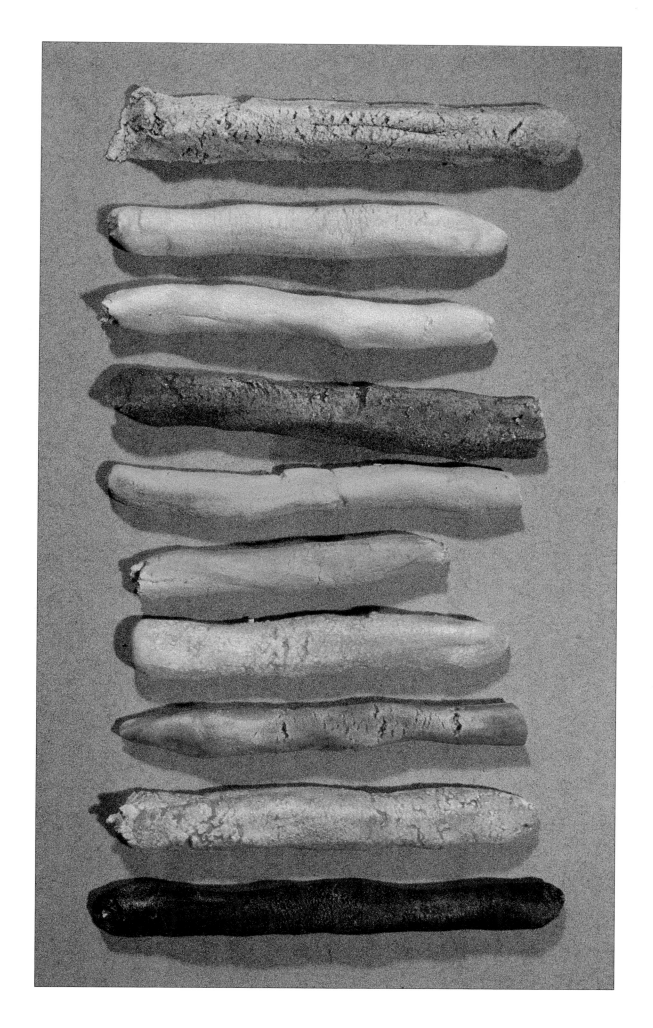

9. Sketching a street scene

The town or city is an ideal place for sketching; there are always endless subjects to look at and choose from, there is colour and vitality, buildings of a hundred different colours and shapes, details like a curious window railing or an unusual brickwork facade, brightly coloured doors and window frames, crisp black lines of cast iron railings. Or think of office tower blocks, soaring into the air like medieval cathedrals – sometimes sited all too near the cathedral to the detriment of both. Don't overlook the charm of small cottage-like buildings tucked away in almost all our towns, some with irregular beams framing lead-casement windows. A few are truly ancient, some are Victorian or even modern adaptations, and after you have spent hours drawing the fine details you'll be able to tell the difference very quickly.

Towns are good for having plenty of nooks and crannies to set up your easel; unused doorways give you ample protection against the weather as well as the passing crowds (but not in front of someone's garage!) or prop your back against a stone wall while you draw. When the weather is cold or wet, think about drawing from an office window. Assuming you have permission to be there, you'll be able to sit in comfort and watch the world outside as if it were a stage.

If you add figures to your sketch, remember that you won't be able to paint them slowly as if they were standing still. Look at the person once, fix the image in your mind, and then sketch them in quickly without following them as they walk on past.

Of course, the obvious and easiest medium is a pad of paper and a pencil, a small box of watercolours, or a selection of felt pens. Look for strong sunlight coming from the side; it creates dark shadows on the facades and the window frames. Oils and pastels can be used, but you really need so much more equipment that I would keep them for very quiet weekends when there is little or no traffic, few people about, and you can settle down with a chair and easel for a morning or afternoon.

10. Lighting a model

In an earlier project we looked at all the different ways light can affect the composition of a still-life painting. Lighting is even more complex and exciting when the composition is built around the human figure.

Too many art and photography books tend to look at lighting the figure as if it were an inanimate object. A model is a human being, clothed or unclothed, as much of an individual as the sitter for a portrait.

Of course we need to keep the flexibility of seeing forms, colours and shapes as well as acknowledging that this is a human being. Only complete abstraction is successful in taking us right away from the human reference to a simple geometric reality, and then lighting is not one of the most obvious problems the artist will have.

Variations on light sources

We are used to seeing people with top light or overall light, such as sunlight; this gives a simple, clear definition, showing details and colouring but also cutting down heavily on the atmosphere and emotional effect.

Think of the grotesquerie in a face lit from below, the mystery in the candle-lit portrait or the magic in the light from an open door, spilling into a dark room and half-lighting a figure in a chair. In fact, any kind of side lighting brings its own psychological effect.

A single, strong, direct light source, especially from the side, can make an exciting picture, creating a high degree of contrast in light and shade. However, this will make the side that is lit seem bleached out, while the dark side will lack any detail or definition.

If you have only one lamp to light your figure, hang some sort of diffusion between the light source and the model — a sheet of muslin or even paper will spread the light sufficiently for most paintings, while still retaining the side-lit effect. An additional lamp, no matter how small, used on the opposite side will make all the difference, just lightening the density enough to create a better balance between the two sides. If you have no access to another light, a sheet of aluminium used as a reflector will catch some of the light and throw it back on to the model.

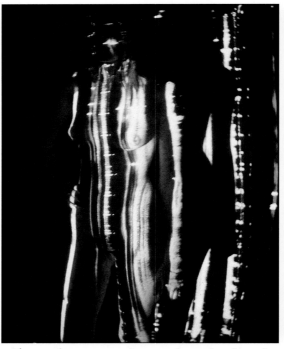

If you have a projector there is also the chance to throw some exotic patterns on to the model. This makes for an exciting project, although it is not very useful in attempting a traditional portrait!

Back lighting — that is positioning the model in front of a light source, such as a window or a strongly lit wall — will give you some fascinating effects; the model appears in silhouette, and if the painting is concentrating on the shape of the figure rather than the face it is an interesting variation to try.

Front lighting — that is, the source coming from behind the artist — is another way of experimenting. This will tend to flatten out all the depth and modelling of the face and figure, as does a built-in flash on a camera, and the three-dimensional effect of reality is greatly diminished. This, of course, can be used deliberately when you want to concentrate on pattern and colour rather than form.

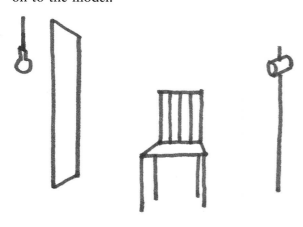

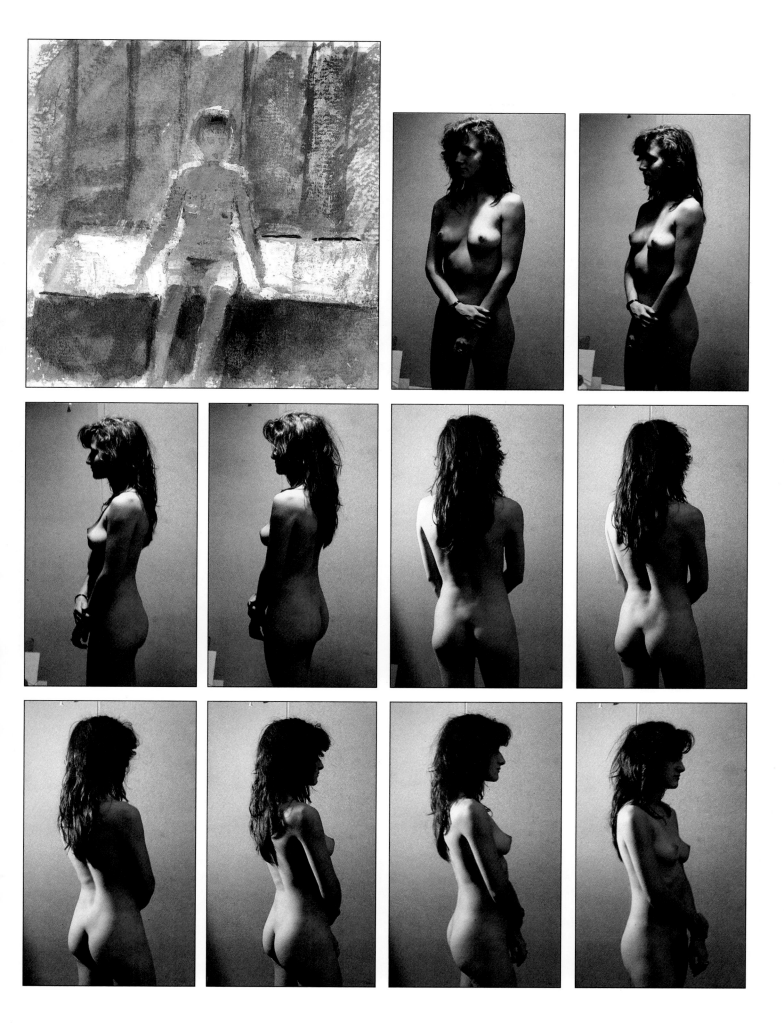

Day-Long Projects

1. A trip to the seaside
2. Making the most of museums
3. Designing and building a storage rack
4. Painting the nude
5. Glazes in watercolour and oil
6. Looking at a building
7. High key and low key
8. A pointillist study in watercolour
9. Flower studies
10. Working with collage

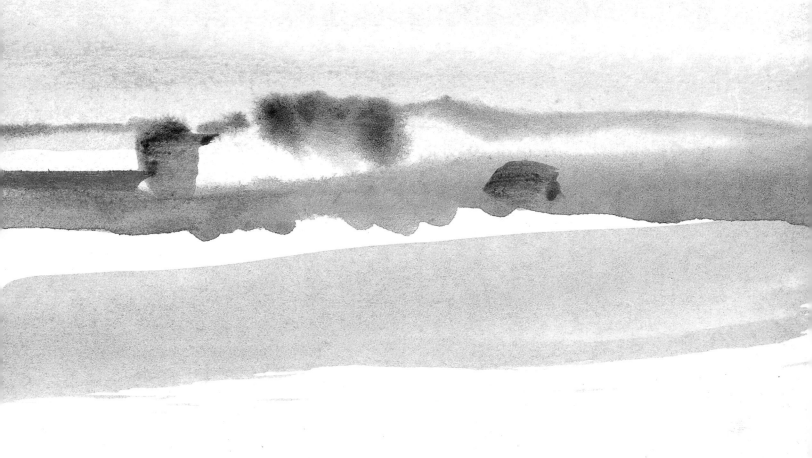

Tom Rm.

1. A trip to the seaside

One of the most popular excursions a painter can make must surely be to a seaside town. It's so rich in possibilities; the bleak coastal shapes and muted neutral colours of sand dunes, the bright pastels and crisp black and white of the promenade, the wrought-iron railings and curly benches. There's the sea, of course, across the horizon or beyond a lighthouse. A busy resort is quiet early in the morning, with just a few residents walking their dogs, yet crowded later with holidaymakers and children. The beach itself, with striped deck chairs and kiosks piled high with coloured balls and hoops, offers a riot of colour. Along the harbour there may be a sleek white cruising yacht or a few battered, rough, fishing boats; and perhaps nearby there are deserted estuaries, shimmering with rock pools and reed-filled ponds graced by spindle-shanked wading birds. No wonder that seaside painters of today follow a tradition that dates back to the sketches of Constable and Cotman through the marvellous watercolours and oils of Boudin, Courbet and almost all the Impressionists and Post-Impressionists.

Choosing where to go

Establish in your mind what you want to paint today and perhaps what you might want to do another day.

An invaluable aid I use is my painting planner, which lists all the items I should think about beforehand and has a space for all the information I might need.

The ideal is to find somewhere two or three hours' journey from your house; if you make an early start, there's enough time to sketch on the journey as well as at the seaside.

I want to record the whole day and bring home enough material to keep me busy in the studio for at least another week. The great difference between 'a day at the seaside' and an expedition to paint a particular picture is the wide range covered by the project, so you should be prepared for any eventuality.

Easy-to-carry and easy-to-use materials help you to go wherever you like. I have also learned from experience that during the summer I am happier avoiding the problems of oils and crayons (wet paint gets covered in sand and debris from the breeze and wax crayons melt in the sun into a Joseph's coat of many colours), so I take a pad and pencils or pastels for the journey and watercolours for the beach.

Two 2B pencils are enough for sketching on the train, and an HB pencil for roughing in outlines when I move on to a hand-made watercolour paper with a rough surface. If you prefer to paint on smooth cartridge paper, the 2B would do for marking out as well.

If space and weight are a consideration, take one of the tiny watercolour boxes that hold only 8 or 9 colours – quite enough for the limited palette you need. Pans are always better than tubes for quick sketching.

A mixed box of pastels is handy. I have an old cigarette case with an elastic band for holding the cigarettes in place – it makes a perfect pastel or crayon carrier, and they are still easy to find in junk shops.

Take a very small sketchbook for the journey and larger paper or a pad for the beach; a penknife to keep pencils sharp (and for peeling fruit when you get thirsty), a rubber and a rag, a little flask for water. You can make your own holdall or buy a canvas or thin nylon carrier. Look for a top wide enough to take your sketchbooks, a few pockets to hold small items, and sturdy handles.

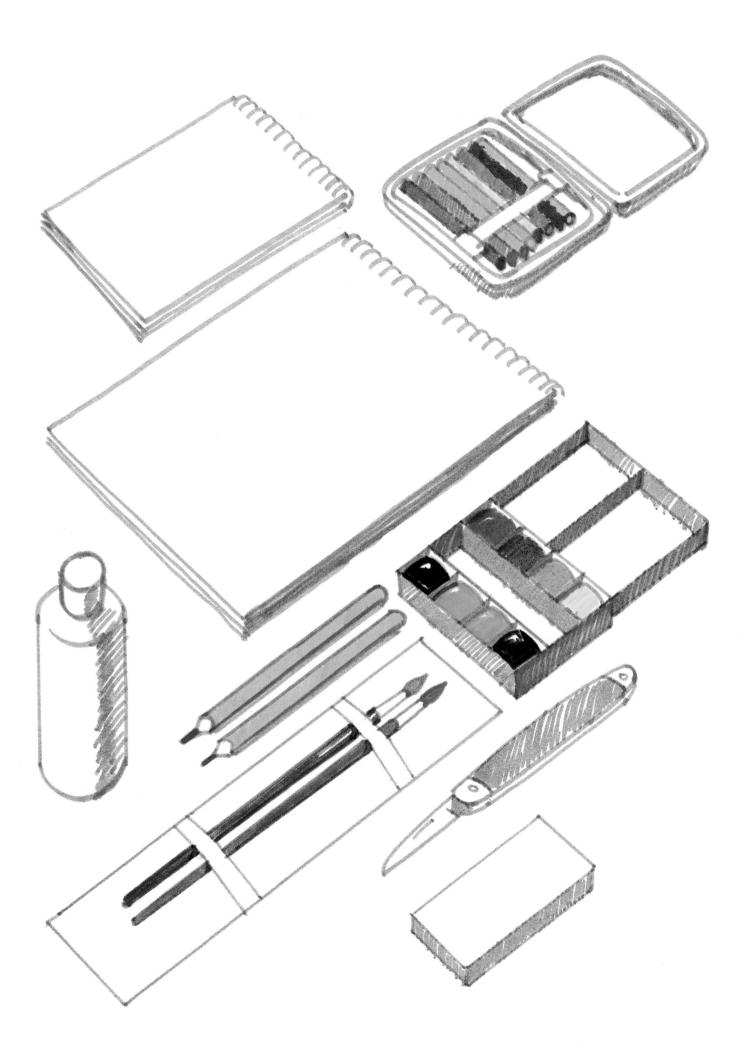

Remember that *sea water must not be used as a mixer* for your watercolour paints; the colours will be badly affected.

I only take one or two brushes rolled up in a thin split-cane place mat; the open-work canes let the brushes dry on the way home.

An easel is unnecessary, but a small folding stool is not much to carry; even if you have a car, it usually has to be parked a long way from where you want to paint. Comfortable clothes and shoes are absolute priorities.

Tuck in some lotion or protective cream — the glare at the seaside can be remarkably strong. Sunglasses should be of neutral density; these will change tone but not colour. Ordinary sunglasses will tint everything brown or blue. A hat is a good idea; a peak or brim will shade your head as well as your eyes.

Carry a little water or a drink for yourself, rather than having to depend on finding a café that is not too crowded and near enough to where you want to paint.

Finally, there is usually quite a breeze on the coast, almost always gusty and sometimes surprisingly chilly; a light windbreaker can come in handy, especially late in the day.

On the way

Painting is like any other activity; it benefits from warming-up exercises. A new day, a new view of things — the hand and eye need a little practice to get together. If your journey is by train or bus it's easy — you can make sure you have a sketch pad and pencil, and keep it busy all the time. If you are going by car, carrying equipment is no problem; stop now and then to look at the view, to make a sketch or two, just sitting by the roadside, to take a photograph of a morning sky, or a field of glowing corn; you are psyching yourself up for the main work of the day.

There's no point in trying to do fine, detailed work in a moving vehicle; you'll be jogged up and down. If you will be travelling by car, buy suction cup holders that cling to the window from a car accessory shop — they will hold enough water for at least two or three sketches.

I sometimes use the windscreen as a frame, and the driving mirror becomes part of the painting.

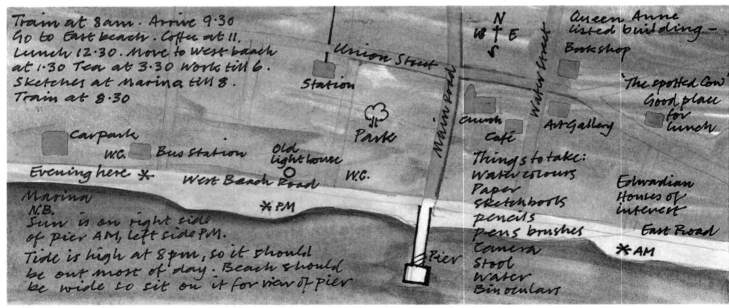

Train at 8am. Arrive 9.30
Go to East beach. Coffee at 11.
Lunch 12.30. Move to West beach
at 1.30 Tea at 3.30 Works till 6.
Sketches at Marina till 8.
Train at 8.30

Car park
W.C. Bus Station Old light house Park
Evening here * West Beach Road W.C.
Marina
N.B.
Sun is on right side
of pier AM, left side PM.
Tide is high at 8pm, so it should
be out most of day. Beach should
be wide to sit on it for view of pier
* PM

Station
Union Street
N
W + E
S
Main Road
church Water Street Café Art Gallery
Things to take:
Water colours
Paper
Sketchbooks
pencils
pens brushes
Camera
stool
water
Binoculars
Pier

Queen Anne
listed building —
Bookshop
'The spotted Cow'
Good place
for lunch
Edwardian
Houses of
interest
East Road
* AM

At the beach

Finding a really intriguing subject is first on the list; if you have done your homework there are clues everywhere, even if you've never been to the place before. This is how it worked out for me on a day in the summer.

A note in the town guide mentioned the beach huts, and a short walk found this delightful scene, the line of multi-coloured huts stretching away down the beach. It was the perfect time of day – not crowded yet, but with enough people around to add sparkle.

To see how the scene would fill the paper I sketched in the line of the roofs, and then the main features, in very light pencil, plotting where I intended to use white or clear colours. It is easier to avoid covering those places with washes now rather than having to do a lot of lifting off later.

Soon the beach began to fill up, but I decided to keep the early-morning feeling by limiting the number of figures. A trained memory means you can go on painting what you first saw, but if the new arrivals make a more interesting picture, then adapt your composition or start again.

In the hot sun, the washes of blue and umber dried in a few minutes. I used just a dash of pigment each time to a lot of water.

When I started on the beach huts, the process was reversed; I used only a little water so that the colours stayed separate. I left white spaces just below the roofs to give the impression of reflected sunlight.

Doors, windows and so on were added only after the first washes were absolutely dry. Finally the people, screens and towels were put in with a few brushstrokes here and there.

To erase all traces of the pencil use a rubber only after the paper is bone dry, working carefully and lightly so you don't lift any of the paint or the surface of the paper.

In the afternoon I decided to make a sketch of the pier, glittering with its new white paint. This went much more quickly, with just a few basic washes, and a soft grey to add shape to the stones of the wall, the deck chairs, the heads of the figures, the shadow in the foreground and under the boat, and the standing figures here and there. A single brush of viridian green for the trees, a few strokes of blue and orange for the figures and pier towers and it was finished.

Learning to look at a scene and see it in simple washes like this is the best way to appreciate the quality of the medium.

While you have the opportunity, look for

unusual angles and subjects for smaller, individual sketchbook vignettes. I took a fancy to a pattern of waves and grains of sand rendered in pastels; next a boat, set up on its blocks and making black and white shapes against the sky, caught my eye.

Going home

Slip the sketches into the watercolour pad for protection. Wash out the brushes (*not in sea water!*) and roll them up; they will dry quickly inside their protective mat. Felt pens should be carefully capped and pastels slipped away into their case. Rubbish should be thrown away in the litter bins; many people don't realize that paint can be toxic to animals.

I always keep sketching, even on the way home; people are often half asleep and that makes them easy to draw!

Once home, there are still things to do; I tidy up and put the sketches away, looking at them again to decide if I caught the moment or the effect I was looking for. I might be disappointed, in which case I'll want to try a scene or a special effect another day. Remember always to make notes in your painting diary.

Painting is a continual activity, and it becomes a way of life. Your mind doesn't stop thinking about shapes, colours and forms the minute you put down your brush. To get the best out of the day, let yourself wind down a little from the tension of looking and learning, gradually relaxing with a new and richer storehouse of ideas and images.

2. Making the most of museums

The first visit to any museum or exhibition is a signal to put aside all the art history and background learned over the years. Too much information too soon, and you end up seeing what you expect or hope to see instead of what is on the wall in front of you.

Every painting, no matter how familiar or famous, deserves the effort of a fresh approach. And that is exactly what museums can offer – personal, direct experience. Of course there are other ways to enjoy paintings: first-class printed reproductions give a reasonable approximation of the real thing; books can explain history and context; films and television programmes can re-create the time, the place, the influences of an artist's family life. However, it's only in museums and galleries that we are able to come face to face with the greatest artists; one human being has created an image, another looks and responds.

When the observer is also a painter, however new and amateur or experienced and professional, the response broadens immediately. The problems an artist confronts every day have remained the same for centuries, and the solutions already found are ones we have to discover for ourselves; brushstrokes can be traced on the surface to teach us something about direction and impact, colours teach a lesson in compatibility or contrast, shapes are a new language in space and dimension. Concentrating on the fabric of a painting is a way of seeing through the eyes and following the hand of the artist.

Left: Simon de Vleigal
Right: Von Rysselburgh

Project

If it is a collection that you haven't seen before, begin your day by walking through the entire gallery, slowly enough to look at the various groupings and sections, but without stopping at any picture for more than a minute or two.

Then sit down somewhere quietly and decide which group you want to look at carefully, and why. In a large gallery you are going to have to curb your enthusiasm a little – if you try to see everything in one day you'll end up with sore feet, blurred vision and a woolly head.

If the gallery covers the entire history of art, choose a period – perhaps all the Dutch painters of the 16th and 17th centuries. If it features a particular period, choose an artist within that period. If it's a one-man show, look at part of the artist's work; landscapes or early paintings, portraits or still lifes.

Go around again, without a catalogue and without looking (if you can restrain yourself) at the names or titles on the frames.

Look for paint handling, for rough or careful brushstrokes, and the unmistakable marks of the palette knife; for oil paintings so layered in glazes they are as smooth as glass, or sketches drawn right on the canvas in bright areas of colour. Look for the variety of underpainting – many paintings in need of repair give you a chance to see beneath the surface where it has flaked away. A great pity for the preservation of the painting itself, but it is fascinating to learn a little more about how the canvas was primed, what colour was used, and so on.

Look for the way watercolours have been laid on in washes and dry brush. Look for places where the paper was left white, and where touches of gouache white were added to the surface. Look for the control of pigment bleeding wet into wet, and for the very precise handling of miniature details.

Look for colours; for high-key and low-key paintings, for the attempt to create natural effects so that trees are shades of green, faces tones of flesh colour, and for those paintings where the colours have been deliberately altered; green faces, elongated purple bodies.

Look for space and dimension; flat landscapes with cardboard figures one behind the other, or complicated and oversized crowd scenes that seem to stretch for miles into the

distance – and all the subtleties in between.

When you are at an exhibition by more than one artist, you'll be able to compare the way each individual used the tools of art to make a personal statement. Even when the painters seem to work in almost identical ways, close study usually shows up their own adaptation of the media.

By now it should be time to stop for lunch. If it is a large collection, it will be a late lunch! Try to go out if you can; you want to restore your eye, rest your brain, and refresh your sense of pleasure.

After lunch, find a quiet spot again somewhere in the gallery where you can get up from time to time and look at something that catches your eye. Read through the catalogue if there is one available, without trying to memorize every fact.

Pick out three paintings, no more, that you really enjoyed looking at. Find any information there is on them in the catalogue or in handbooks in the museum store. Go back to each painting in turn with the morning's impression fresh in your mind, and try to put together the technical knowledge you were able to absorb from the background or critical comments you read subsequently.

Finally, make notes for yourself in the diary at home about what you saw and what you thought interesting – or boring or overrated. Write down any queries about technique or historical influence, so that you can follow them up later; appreciation and enjoyment are built on an accumulation of little moments of understanding.

Left: The Duc de Bourgogne Right, clockwise from the top: Henri Matisse, Odilon Redon, René Magritte, Paul Klee and Pierre Bonnard

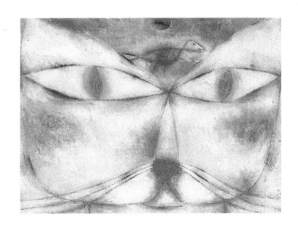

3. Designing and building a storage rack

Even if you are a beginner you will soon acquire quite a few paintings. You may not think they are very successful, but you can learn an enormous amount from failures as well as successes and a storage rack makes a very instructive chamber of horrors. Later, when you start to produce work that you are proud of, you will want to keep it safe.

There are some conditions to be avoided; dampness is perhaps the biggest problem. Many studios, especially spare rooms in a house or a flat, are not heated all year round; they tend to be colder and damper than the rest of the house. As a precaution, avoid putting your rack against an outside wall.

The other major problem is dust, or fumes from boilers, cookers, flues, etc. Open coal fires and continual cigarette or pipe smoke really do have an appalling effect on all art works.

You can keep work in polythene bags, but this isn't really a good idea except for short periods – perhaps during spring cleaning, or when it is being carried back and forth to an exhibition. They are particularly unsuitable for pastels; the bags do protect their delicate surface but the flakes rub off eventually and then get transferred to other parts of the picture.

Any sort of industrial or workshop dust is especially dangerous, so keep DIY enthusiasts away from the studio.

Oil painting storage

Oil paintings need air circulating around them to stay in reasonable condition. The paint is gradually cured as it dries over a period of months or even years. If the paintings are not stored carefully they deteriorate quite quickly and damage occurs in the natural glues of the size, the fibres in the canvas, the gums in the oil and, of course, the wood of the stretchers. When they are badly stacked, there is also the very real danger of one canvas pushing a hole through another, or one surface being abraded by the canvas on top of it.

Canvases leaning against a wall are reasonably safe, but it becomes quite a feat to move each pile to find what you want.

Vertical storage in a damp-free environment gives you the best protection, with enough divisions to contain up to only a dozen paintings in each section.

Watercolour storage

Watercolours are also subject to damp and mildew, and while new paintings can be pinned up in your studio for quite a time, they will eventually deteriorate and fade as the colours are bleached by the light and the paper begins to collect dust and greasy marks from fingerprints. Unless you are going to frame the painting very soon it is best to store it flat as soon as it is bone dry – usually a matter of minutes, but very occasionally a few hours or even a day when the weather is particularly cold or damp.

Even if they are kept carefully in an ordinary portfolio watercolours can become faded and yellow, and the paper can break up around the edge. Horizontal shelves and acid-free tissue paper will separate each layer and protect them all from dust.

Positioning the rack

Ideally, any rack should be on an inside wall, well away from direct sunlight or dust. An inner alcove in a studio, or across the wall in a small room, is a suitable place; across the top of a doorway, taking advantage of unused space, is a good solution as long as you keep a pair of steps handy to climb up when you want something.

Design for an oil painting rack

The rack is 5 ft (152 cm) long by 2 ft 10 inches (86 cm) high, giving storage space of 4 ft 2 inches (127 cm) – enough for roughly 48 paintings at a maximum width of 1 inch (2.5 cm) for each canvas (most are only ¾ inch (19 mm) wide, and the extra allows for sliding in and out).

This method is confined to simple screw and glue for both racks to make it absolutely straightforward, with no mitred joints.

This is a basic shape, adaptable to any length and almost any height, always using 2 × 2 inch (50 × 50 mm) timber. You will need to pin it to the wall along the top rail for extra strength – four wall plugs and long screws should do.

The rack doesn't fit tightly against the back wall – this is to allow air to circulate, and it is important that you leave that gap free.

A cover can be easily made by hanging a sheet of plastic or fabric like a curtain over the front, perhaps even attached to a simple curtain wire with hooks and eyes at each end.

A working surface can be added to the top of the rack by fitting a plain piece of laminated chipboard. If the rack has to be built in a family room and you want to hide it more effectively, simply make the working surface a little deeper than the rack so it overhangs the edge about ½ inch (12 mm), add a pretty curtain to match the rest of the furnishings and it will look like a dressing table or sideboard.

Watch out for the danger of it becoming a kind of family catch-all; if dusty or damp objects are piled on top the paintings inside might be damaged.

I have built my rack inside the studio as one tall unit, but the two racks could stand side by side to give a long working surface.
Variations:
1(a) A small set of extra bars in the last section can provide two smaller racks for small canvases.
1(b) The first section without its front rail will provide storage for very tall paintings.
1(c) A rack that offers all together.
1(d) Combination oil and watercolour.

Making the rack

The timber is lengths of basic 2 × 2 inch (50 × 50 mm) pine or deal.

The finished lengths will be a little less than when you pick the timber up from the lumber yard, so if you are making the rack to fit exactly into a particular space, take the measurements along to the yard for final checking.

You will need:
4 × 5 ft (152 cm) lengths for long struts
10 × 2 ft 10 inch (86 cm) lengths for uprights
10 × 14 inch (35 cm) lengths for connectors
68 × 3 inch (76 mm) screws (No. 10), using 3 for each joint, 8 for wall-pinning and batten
PVA wood glue

Lay two long rails on the ground, and put the five uprights in position on top of them (see diagram). Make sure, with a T-square or just a piece of right-angled card, that they are square.

Drill the screw holes for the end pairs of uprights right through them and into the long rails for about ½ inch (12 mm). Coat the two surfaces with PVC and screw them together. This is your back frame. Mark where the wall fixings are going to be and drill through the wood.

Repeat these steps so that you now have the front and back frames exactly alike except for the holes for the wall fitting, which are only on the back rail.

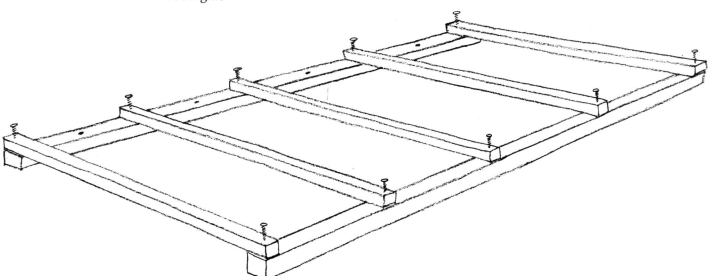

Fix the back frame to the wall. You may need to clear the skirting board by screwing an equally thick batten of wood to the wall at the height of the top rail, and affixing the rack to this.

If you think there might be pipes or wires running behind the wall go carefully; tapping through a very thin nail before you drill is a good precaution. (If you plan to build fitted studio furniture there are new DIY machines which will show where there are waterpipes or electrical conduits in the walls.)

Drill two holes right through all the shortest pieces of wood, 1 inch (2.5 cm) from each end.

Put glue on the ends of the short lengths, and on the rails and the uprights, and screw all the short rails to the back frame, starting at the bottom.

All the joints work exactly the same way. Only the right-hand short connecting lengths are set differently, on the inside of the last two uprights.

Then slide the front into position and glue and screw that to the connecting short pieces.

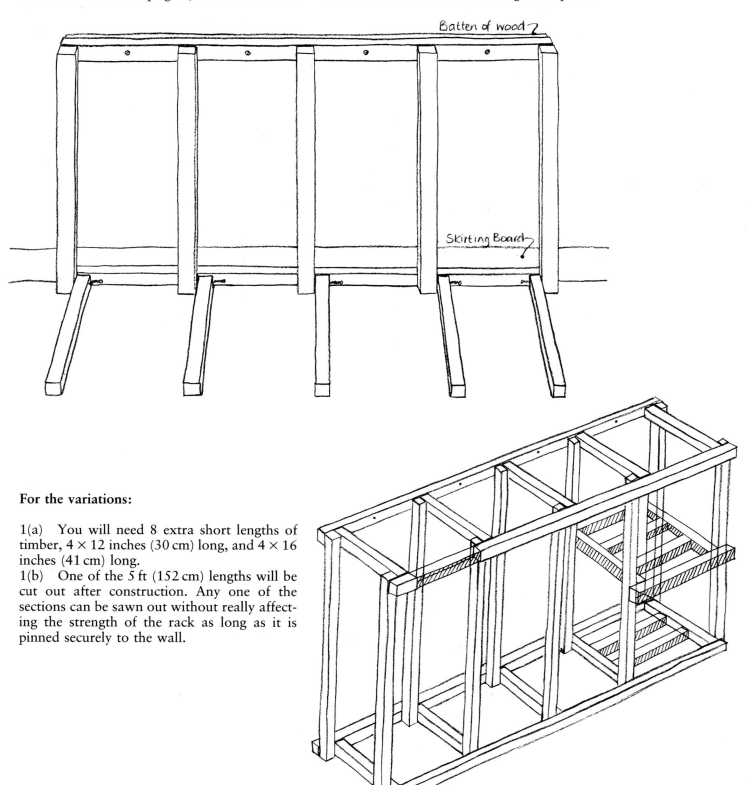

For the variations:

1(a)   You will need 8 extra short lengths of timber, 4 × 12 inches (30 cm) long, and 4 × 16 inches (41 cm) long.

1(b)   One of the 5 ft (152 cm) lengths will be cut out after construction. Any one of the sections can be sawn out without really affecting the strength of the rack as long as it is pinned securely to the wall.

Making a watercolour rack

The storage in this version is basically horizontal rather than vertical, and closed rather than open-shelved, for maximum protection against dust.

If the rack is to be fixed to the wall, you may not need a back; add extra support with little brass picture plates along the top edge. Remember the skirting board; if you have one, you'll need a batten along the wall to go under the top rail.

To avoid going to the trouble of making doors, fit a curtain to keep the paintings inside free from dust. Even a bit of net is better than nothing. In a living room, you can match up fabric from the curtains or chairs so the rack blends into the general decor.

All construction is in ½ inch (12 mm) chipboard planks 18 inches (45 cm) wide.

For our model, which is 4 ft (121 cm) overall long and 18 inches (45 cm) wide, you will need:
2 × 4 ft (121 cm) lengths
2 × 3 ft 11 inch (119 cm) lengths
2 × 2 ft 6 inch (76 cm) lengths
3 × 9⅓ inch (23.5 cm) lengths
30 × 1 inch (25 mm) panel pins
PVA wood glue

Follow all the steps for the first rack; the only difference is in the front.

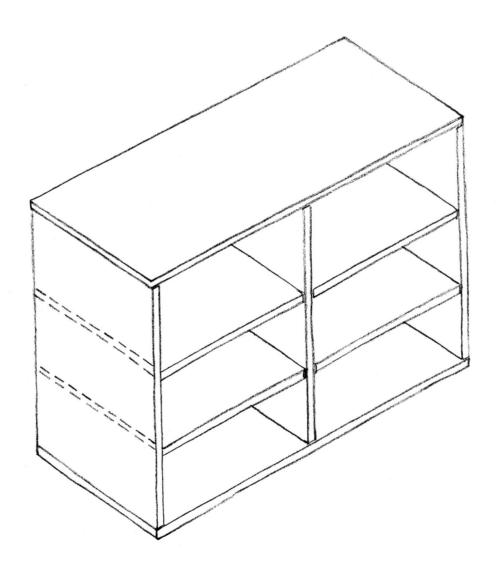

4. Painting the nude

The human figure is fascinating to us all. From a very early age, the shapes and feelings of our own bodies are what we know best, and what we experience most keenly and continually. We like to look at other people, too, recognizing that the human body in all its many forms is the most complex and yet the most satisfying object imaginable.

Art teachers often forget, though, that there are many inhibitions about looking at nude bodies, and new art students in particular often need a certain amount of encouragement to appreciate that figure studies are a very necessary element in learning to paint.

Finding a model

In an emergency you could use your own body as a model, but that creates physical problems; trying to sit comfortably and see yourself at the same time can destroy your concentration.

Finding a model is by far a better solution. A wife or husband is a good choice; at least it provides the framework of an easy relationship which avoids awkwardness at the first sittings.

If you work with other painters, that can solve most of the practical problems; by chipping in to make up a life class of your own you can afford to pay for a professional model each time – or you can take turns posing yourselves, each contributing one session.

Notes for setting up

Daylight brings out the subtle contrasts of skin, although you may need an extra lamp or two. As this is an all-day project, choose a north-lit room if you can so that the light stays relatively constant throughout the project.

Decide where the model is going to sit. You will need a clean chair or a bed or even the floor, covered with a cloth. The room must be warm, without draughts, and you may need a portable heater to keep the temperature even during the day. There should be a changing area – a room or a screen with a hanger, a chair and some kind of dressing-gown available. A professional model will bring his or her own.

For the background, it's pleasant to have extra cushions and fabrics around to try out against the skin and hair. Simple, strong colours are always effective, but muted pastels can also be good, especially if your model is very fair and you want to keep the picture soft and gentle in appearance. Don't choose an antique shawl or a valuable silk throw because you will want to mark the position of the model with chalk or charcoal before he or she moves.

Put the easel in a comfortable position so that you can see the model at the side without having to keep shifting your head and body. You also want the easel to catch the light, so angle it in relation to the light source.

The model should be sitting in a comfortable position in a warm and comfortable environment. A pose which allows for knitting or reading is a nice idea, making him or her feel at home.

Try out a few poses yourself so that when the model comes in you can demonstrate exactly what you want. It is almost impossible to describe the nuances of a pose in words; if you can take up the pose the model will be able to copy you easily.

Models need a break; a professional model will pose for up to 40–45 minutes, and then take a 15-minute break. Amateurs will certainly need shorter posing times, no longer than 30 minutes, and perhaps even 20, with 10-minute breaks.

Before the model has the first break you must 'mark' the pose. This means drawing with chalk around the feet, the backside, the hands, and anything else that touches the support. Remember to mark the position of the chair or bed itself on the floor and, if the easel might have to be moved, mark that on the floor, too.

The break must be used for walking around to get the circulation going again. If new models feel like going on, they may surprise themselves and everyone else by fainting! Of course, the painters can continue working on the background or refining some small detail while the model is resting.

Encourage the model to be interested in the progress of the various paintings – it adds to a pleasant atmosphere in the studio. Payment, if appropriate, is made at the end of the session, usually by the hour, sometimes by the day. Check with your local art school for current rates.

A day's painting

Right: A few simple variations on placing the model.

First Session

10.30: Rough in the composition, filling the whole canvas. I use blue-grey paint for an outline. If you are not sure about the pose or your placement of the easel move around the room, blocking in quick oil sketches to see how the figure fills the canvas from different directions. Once you are satisfied about the placement, try another two sketches in black and white to see what happens when you change the light source.

121

11.15: Time for a break and a stretch. If there are a few of you painting, appoint someone to keep an eye on the clock. When you all get carried away you'll have a fainting model all too soon!

You can go on working during the break, sketching in the background, the fabrics and the floor; they give emphasis and strength to the composition.

Second Session

11.30–12.15: Using a fine brush, refine the drawing, going over the first outlines. Work accurately this time, leaving space for details and patterns. Look for proportions and articulation – the arms and legs should bend naturally and the head should be in proportion to the body.

12.30–1.30: Lunch. You and the model both need a break, in your case to let what you are doing simmer in your head. Go out, if possible, so you can come back with a fresh eye. Remember to make sure the model can find something to eat nearby, or provide a few sandwiches and a drink yourself.

Third Session

1.30–2.15: Make a final assessment of the colours and rough in all the basic ones. This will be part of the finished picture, so work carefully over the whole canvas.

Fourth Session

2.30–3.15: All the secondary colours and tones should be added now, with modulations and changes in light and shade.

3.15–4.00: Tea or coffee break. Go out of the room so that your eye will come back full of other images and find the painting as if it were new.

Final Session

4.00–4.45: Add the final details of drawing and pattern, splashes of colour, and highlights in the face and body to give the final sparkle.

You can go on working for a few days on background details, but try not to work on the figure without the model. Very often chopping and changing only makes things worse; if you are really unhappy about the picture, it might be better to start all over again the following week.

Painting the figure is one of the most difficult crafts. You have only to look at the work of the great masters, at their studies in anatomy, texture and composition, and at their endless, endless sketching to appreciate that this is not something to be mastered in a few lessons.

Be pleased with having made a start!

Left and right: sketches with alternate lighting. The same picture in a watercolour sketch, showing how easy it is to use alternate mediums.

Overleaf: The painting at the end of the day. When you are working in oil you can go on and on for a week or more, experimenting, adding a few touches, taking away some lines which bother you. Here I think that in a few days I would like to increase the detail in the background and in the model's face, and perhaps add a little warmer blue to the right-hand corner.

5. Glazes in watercolour and oil

The first techniques developed for the new medium of oil were adapted from the older medium of watercolour, especially the use of thin glazes to create subtle changes and shadows, cooling or warming a palette as the picture progressed. The only real change in practical terms was the venue; watercolour glazes could be put on outdoors, if necessary, while oil glazes were almost always added in the studio as they took far too long to dry.

All classical painters used glazing as a natural part of their work; I am sure that many of the heavily cleaned pictures in over-bright, almost raw colours have been cleaned right down to the underpainting. All the subtle layers of lightly toned glazes, or varnishes, that were the final touches have been dissolved by the enthusiastic restorer.

The style of the layered oil painting based on the use of glazes lasted well into the 19th century, but as soon as direct painting outdoors became fashionable oil glazes were used less and less. The reintroduction of many traditional forms of landscape and still life has brought back glazing as a technique, however. In the modern art world, direct painting outdoors is generally practised by only a few professional painters, although it retains an enormous appeal for amateurs at all levels.

The use of acrylic has also stimulated interest in this very old tradition because of its ability to be applied in thin, quick-drying layers. The artist can now continue to work without waiting for days or weeks between each application.

Perhaps another contribution to the revival has been the demand for painted finishes in home decoration, as a result of which there are all kinds of glaze products and commercial mixes easily available.

Basic technique

The layers are built up on a base of opaque ground (in oil this is produced by underpainting, in watercolour it may be underpainting or the paper itself which may be opaque) using glaze, or varnish, mixed with paint to give a gradated transparent effect. This results in a much richer colour than it is possible to achieve with paint thinned with oil or turpentine.

Top glazes (which are usually referred to in modern terms as the varnishing) are laid on in broad washes, often 'wiped out' in places and even overpainted to give extra dimension to highlights. 'Wiping out', or lifting the glaze from the surface with a brush or rag dipped in turpentine, is used in glazing as a positive statement, not a cure for mistakes.

Examples:
1. Rag rolling. Raw umber mixed with varnish has been painted on and then rolled over with a crumpled soft rag to give a texture like rocks or drapery.
2. 'Wiping out.' The thick base has been overglazed with raw umber, which has then been wiped off to leave highlights.
3. The sky is a blue glaze, wiped off the canvas to leave white, just like washing out in watercolour.

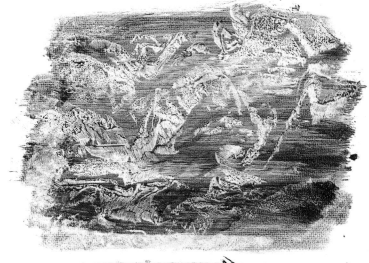

4. The fish are painted in many layers of thin, transparent glaze; the last layer is brushed on over the whole painting so that the effect is of seeing the objects underneath water. It is not possible to achieve this illusion in any other way.

6. Looking at a building

All human beings have a considerable knowledge of architecture, simply because we live and work in buildings. Although we usually take them for granted they are very complex and interesting places, involving space, shape, form, proportion, geometry, decoration, colour, and even emotional response.

This project is based on making a documentary study of one particular building by doing a series of sketches, designs and drawings.

It can be compared to the study of anatomy; it isn't absolutely necessary, because if you can learn to draw what you see your representation of the building, or of the human figure, should be accurate enough. It will, however, make it much easier to appreciate how buildings are constructed, so that you will be able to sketch them much more accurately when you are in your studio, perhaps working from a photograph.

In theory, you can base your drawings on something as tiny as a summerhouse or as grand as a cathedral. However, life will be easier if you start with something a little more reasonable; a small house or church which you can walk through, look at, and measure inside and out is ideal. You must be able to see and reach at least two, and preferably three, sides. You should also be able to see the front of the building face on, and to find a spot far enough away to see the whole structure as a mass.

Choose a clear day, but preferably without a great deal of harsh sunlight or strong cloud patterns; when there is deep shadow, or the sun is very much at an angle, your eye line will be distorted and it will be very difficult to see details and proportions.

Approaches to consider

Artist's drawings
Sketch plans
Details – windows, doors, ornamentation
Special features
Drawing of the building in its setting

Equipment

A sheet of graph paper
A long tape measure (one that retracts itself is best)
Any hard pencil and a rubber
A small box of coloured pencils or pastels
A drawing pad for details

The first requirement is an appreciation of scale. Begin by establishing the size of the building. There should be at least one side which you can measure along the outside. Put the line down on the graph paper, using a scale of one to three or, in a big building, one to ten.

Then try to judge the height of the outside wall by how it looks compared to the base. If you can get inside, measure the width of the windows and from the floor to their sills; when you go back to your outside drawing those measurements will help you to get the rest of the side, or elevation, in proportion.

Remember that inside there must be enough space between the windows for walls, ceiling levels and so on. Then add quick notes about the doors, windows, roofs, etc. (see diagram).

You are creating an artist's measured drawing – quite enough for your studies, but obviously nowhere near as precise a record as an architectural student would need.

Make a ground-floor plan next. Walk through as much of the building as possible, working from the central hall or the front rooms through to the rear. If it is a small house you can use your tape measure, otherwise just pace it out with strides. Again, remember to add enough space for internal walls, and see if you can find extra supports like beams, columns, etc, which will give you an insight into how the building was constructed.

IMAGINARY DECORATED CHURCH (14 cent

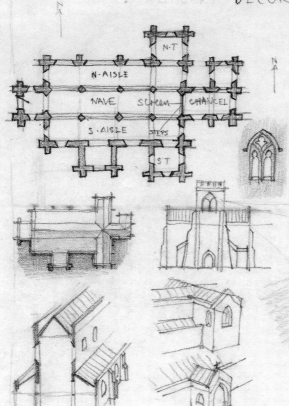

N. T

N. AISLE

NAVE   SCREEN   CHANCEL

S. AISLE   STEPS

S. T

Pointed Decorated arches. Walls thiner,
windows larger, hence flying buttresses.
Roof 45°. Open rafters. imaginative
carving on capitals.
Spire & pinacles.

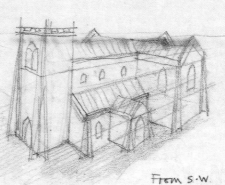

From S.W.

D

IMAGINARY PERPENDICULAR CHIRCH   15th cent

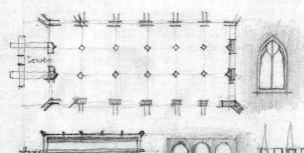

tower

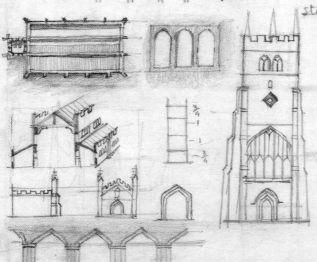

Tower & poarch from Kendal, windows from
Greystoke & plan from Old Baising.
Windows flatened at top, rectangular plan,
roof 36° hiden behind parapet.
Battlements. Doors have square Loodmolding
staned glass windows.

From   FROM S.W

House at Keswick

Keswick

Make some notes for yourself on how the building functions. Do the rooms open into each other or into a central hall? How do the windows in the front relate to the windows at the back? Were the four exterior walls built as different façades or are they all identical? Were the rooms fitted into the need for symmetrical windows on the outside, or do the windows and doors reflect the needs of the inhabitants?

Now you can begin to make detailed drawings of the fascinating touches that every building, no matter how small, contains; glazing patterns in the window, mouldings on the ceiling or around the doors and so on. Coloured surfaces can be roughed in with pencils or pastels.

Finally, having seen inside the bones of the building, make another quick sketch of it from the street. You should be able to appreciate how your new knowledge helps you to see the building much more clearly, making the last sketch easy and enjoyable.

7. High key and low key

Colour is described as having tonal value as well as hue, even though tone refers only to the range of gradations between black and white. The key of a painting or drawing is its tonal character – i.e. the range of tones between the lightest and the darkest.

All pictures fall into some tonal category. Many use the whole range, from purest white to darkest black, like an orchestra with every instrument playing at one time. A very few are based only on absolute black and absolute white.

There are a great many fine paintings which are deliberately restricted to a smaller range of tonal values with subtle changes within the chosen range rather than abrupt contrasts.

These are called high key when the tones are mid to light and low key when the tones are mid to dark.

When you decide what you want to paint and how you intend to show the subject, you should also think about the tonal range. It can help in the selection of just the right level of colour to make the painting express your intentions. Then, as you define the lightest and the darkest colours, and work only within that scale, you'll find that there is a structure and an outline in your painting right from the beginning.

For example, in a bowl of summer flowers – all yellows, whites, and soft greens – the lightest tone is likely to be a white flower and,

working down from there through the sunlight in the window, the yellow tulips and the pale blue buds, you might find the darkest tone in a mid-green leaf or the shadow under the bowl; this would be a high-key composition.

Paint the same bowl of flowers at night, the table glowing and the white becoming golden, the shadows under the bowl dark brown, and the work moves down into a low-key range.

Use the different keys to add to your technical skills; making high-key and low-key sketches before you settle down to the main painting is a quick and simple way of seeing exactly how you want each colour to relate to the others.

As an extra exercise, find some mid-grey paper which will act as your exact mid-point in the tonal range. Make one sketch using only gradations of charcoal to cover the range from grey to black, then make another, using only white chalk, to give a range from grey up to white.

For this project use black and white film in a polaroid camera (obviously any camera will do, but with polaroid film you will see the results instantly).

Put together a group of objects which you think are high key and another group in low key. Take photographs of each group and see how they relate in tonal values. Then try combining objects from black to white, showing the whole spectrum of tones. Look through the colour illustrations of any book on art, trying to see where the artist has used neither black nor white, where the key is decidedly high, and where it is low.

In the two boating scenes, the lightest colour on the high-key painting is the white sails. In the darker, low-key version the sails are still the lightest colour, but they are now a pale grey blue with no white at all.

If you don't have a camera and can't borrow

one easily, cut out magazine illustrations following the same principle of finding high-key and low-key objects. Paste them together into a collage or a group picture and photocopy the end result; this will also give you black and white tones that represent various colours.

After you have made up a few photographic groupings you can use watercolour to try out some high-key and low-key sketches.

In the two boating scenes, the lightest colour on the high-key painting is the white sails. In the darker, low-key version the sails are still the lightest colour but they are now a pale grey blue with no white at all.

The two oil sketches were done while I was planning the painting of the nude figure on page 120. After looking at the results, I decided that I preferred the high-key composition and went on to paint accordingly.

Here are three examples of how painters can use the different keys to structure the tones and therefore the atmosphere.

Top, employing the whole range from white to black, including light and dark browns and blues. Dramatic, but cheerful.

Above, a very high key picture which is so soft that the mid-tone yellow and green act in this composition as strong focal points.

Left, the same colour scale as the top picture, but without any of the white tones; the grey clouds are the lightest area, the whole atmosphere is sombre and brooding instead of sparkling.

8. A pointillist study in watercolour

There is an element of what came to be termed pointillism in all painting; even medieval artists worked with tiny dots of colour to create vibrant effects, especially in borders and decorative miniatures.

During the late 19th century there were many new ideas about colour, light and vision; by breaking down the optical appearance of green, say, into the components of blue and yellow, the theory was that the human eye, oscillating between the two dots laid close together, would see green, and not just ordinary green but a green with a special vitality and shimmer.

The technique developed rapidly amongst a group of artists in Paris. The most famous were George Seurat and Paul Signac, but many of their contemporaries experimented with the theories – Matisse, van Dongen, Mondrian and Delaunay, for example, all left us a few pointillist works – fascinated by science, thrilled by the new inventions which were being made every day, and delighted to find that their natural preoccupation with colour and light had finally become a major source of interest to scientific researchers.

Using tiny dots and dashes of pigment in primary colours was just one of the techniques which became fashionable, but it created such delightfully pleasant and enduringly popular images that many people today think pointillism is synonymous with impressionism.

In practice, artists soon found that blue and yellow, for example, laid close together do not actually create green in the viewer's eye – in fact Seurat's landscapes are filled with various tones of green on the grass and leaves. Some later paintings are in vivid, harsh tones which Seurat and Signac would never have used.

Like many modern 'isms', pointillism grew quickly, reached a fashionable height just before the turn of the century, and almost as quickly lost ground to the newer and even more radical theory of cubism.

There are still painters today who enjoy using fragmented dots of colour to create visual excitement and shimmering colour, and it is certainly a technique which repays experimentation and personal experience.

Using the pointillist technique

A lamp-lit interior shows some of the wide variety of optical effects that can be created with the pointillist technique.

You will need to mix many gradating tones of the colours you want so you can create shadows and modulations by changing the balance of individual colour dots rather than by smoothly blended brushstrokes.

Hold the brush in the Chinese style, touching the paper lightly at right angles. Work first in light tones, gradually moving to darker and brighter colours as the picture develops. The brush must be as dry as possible, so there is no dripping or blurring of the dots; make absolutely sure that every layer is bone dry before you add the next. When you are changing colours wash the brush out thoroughly in clean water because the technique relies heavily on the clarity and purity of the tone. If that gets muddy, it will end up a grey mess.

9. Flower studies

There is surely no need to explain why everyone enjoys painting flowers. Tucked away in almost every artist's sketchbook are drawings of petals and rose hips or clumps of wildflowers with colour sketches of banks of glorious roses and spring bulbs.

Painting flowers opens up a world of variety and pleasure, often to be found in a very small scale. Try looking at the different yellows on just one stem of goldenrod, or the shadows and shades of red in a single rose. Notice how each bud may have a different shape, each thorn a different angle, each leaf a different texture.

Indoors and out, flowers are with us all year round, undemanding models for the painstaking painter yet full of fleeting blossom for the dashing impressionist. Whatever your method of working a bowl of flowers will fit into the schedule, needing only some fresh water and not too much hot sunlight to stay at their best for a few days, perhaps more.

Flower studies indoors

Start with a simple project; a few daisies in a vase with light coming gently in a window to catch the flickers of white and yellow.

Set the vase on the table against a quiet, plain background. Fill in the area of canvas you want to cover, including that of the flowers. Work very quickly and lightly so that the brown of the table blends up into the blue wall. Now paint with light; add the quick strokes of white and yellow, leaving an impression of space and warmth. A few strokes of darker blue to mark the vase, the stems and the shadow, and it is finished.

Try the same project with daffodils, roses or peonies. Look for simple colours, simple shapes. Work towards an idea of conveying the freshness and charm of country flowers without the background of nature, without necessarily even using green, yet giving an artless and natural effect.

Another way of painting flowers is to pick out a small section of a plant to create an enclosed pattern. This is a very useful exercise in learning to decide what you want to paint from a whole range of possibilities that might be in front of your easel.

When working outdoors you can use a viewing card to isolate the area you think most interesting, but in small paintings you really need to train your eye to do the work of the card. Flowering plants make good material for this because their stems and leaves curl into each other, creating designs of space, shape and colour.

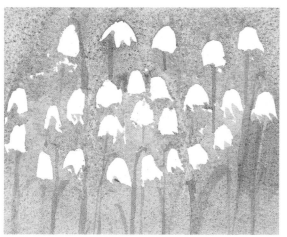

Here are two sketches, one using only tones of green on white, the other a slightly stylized watercolour of the green leaves and white flowers of the bindweed. A gardener regards the bindweed with horror, and sees it as an invader in the garden; a painter can enjoy the incredible suppleness of the stems and the grace of the heart-shaped leaves. Both sketches are the result of narrowing the field of vision to choose just a small section, making that complete within itself. The tone drawing is useful, too, because we concentrate so much on the colour of flowers that we often forget the beauty of their shapes and outlines.

A completely different project involves creating an impression of colour alone. In this pastel drawing of a summer bed of flowers there is no discernible shape or outline; the colours are almost scribbled on to the paper, first the paler background and then a few warmer areas of deeper colour where the blossoms are lightly stroked into place. This approach is based on saturation by waves of colour. Keep your wrist as flexible and light as possible while you work, holding small pieces of the chalk flat on the paper and letting the strokes make their own rhythm on the page.

Finally, try a few portraits of individual flowers, taken completely away from their setting. Use a palette knife to make thick layers of paint which are moulded like the petals or wash on watercolours so delicately that they could almost be dried flowers laid on the page. With the flower pinned to the top of your easel, you won't have to look constantly from the model to your canvas or paper.

10. Working with collage

The word collage is from the French verb *coller*, meaning to stick. It is used to describe a work of art where various materials are added to a flat surface.

Some collages are quite smooth, based on paper scraps, printed pieces, etc., glued down on to the surface so that it is almost impossible to tell whether the design has been painted or stuck on.

Others are much more robust, made up of pieces of wood, metal, *objets trouvés* (found objects), or indeed anything you can think of, held on to the surface by glue or even nails or screws.

A true collage has a painted background; the first known example dates from the beginning of the century, when Picasso glued a piece of patterned oilcloth to the painted image of a kitchen chair. Later the idea was taken up by many Dada and surrealist artists, using a whole range of materials including old bus tickets, photographs of friends and familiar scenes, newspaper clippings and so on.

The advantage of working on collage at least once is the sense of freedom from any technical restrictions. After the tension of holding a pencil or brush for hours, your fingers can relax and enjoy the very different challenge of handling new materials.

Equipment

> A base – a canvas board or a piece of paper
> A good, clear glue that will not stain the fabrics
> An assortment of scraps of fabric, thick papers, magazine cuttings, ribbons, cords, etc.

For a seascape, wash a sheet of watercolour paper in a graduated blue for the sky and a slightly darker blue for the sea.

Complete the picture by using ever scrap of blue material that you can find, fabrics, threads, magazine illustrations, and so on, plus a bit of tissue paper for a white sailing boat. Cut fabrics and paper cleanly with sharp scissors so that the edges don't fray.

Alternatively, try a skyscape made of blue gauze dotted with puffy silk clouds, a landscape containing wooden trains with wheels made of flowers, or simply scraps of paper with pleasant colours and designs.

Make a still life on canvas; try an oil wash undercoat in sepia for the lower half of the painting. Why not find a patterned wallpaper and paste it down to make the background above the sepia 'table'?

Another collage can concentrate on colour. Try a still life made up from scraps of embroidery wool and silk, flakes of wood, flower petals, green wire and leaves.

Finally, an abstract based only on textures; wood and wool, rope and canvas, wax and card, carpet, a leather scrap, crunchy cellophane, lace and sandpaper – anything you have which will provide tactile interest.

Above, collages needn't be flat; use two or three dimensions to make your work stand out.

Right, experiment as much as you can with varied textures on the background as well as on the pieces you glue to the frame.

Above, painted backgrounds can be used for collages; they can be quite recognizable with figures, and symbols, or right, an impressionistic but still quite obvious as a harbour scene with boats.

Week-Long Projects

1. Designing and making a paint box
2. Anatomy
3. Weather: studies in tone
4. Papermaking
5. Texture and detail in still life
6. Problems of the larger composition
7. Nature sketch album
8. Reflections
9. A studio portrait
10. Animals in action

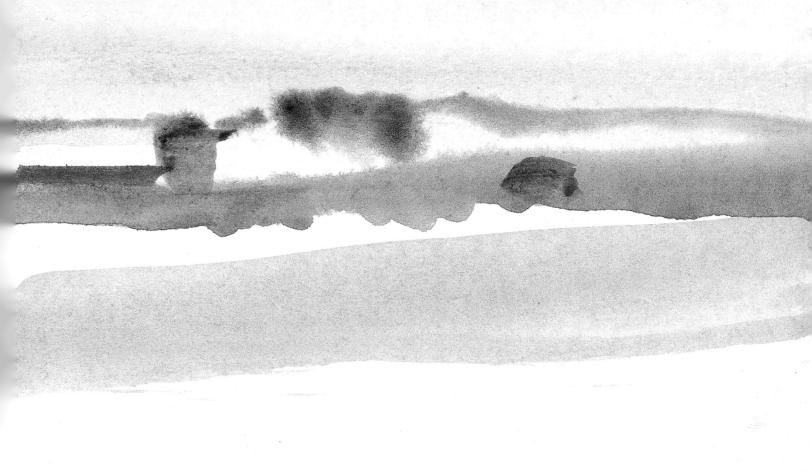

1. Designing and making a paint box

Carrying material in a secure and orderly box is far preferable to letting everything pile up in a carrier bag, getting torn and damaged. Paint boxes come in many different designs, so the first part of the project is to decide exactly what is going to suit you and your personal style of working.

Of course, the absolute minimum requirement is a portable container for your paints and brushes, but here are a few refinements you might consider:

1. Slots to hold a sliding palette, both to work on and slide away after use.
2. Grooves to carry a small canvas inside the lid so that the whole box can be used as a little easel.
3. Collapsible legs which make a table stand for the box, either as an easel or as a stand to hold all your equipment.

Designing the box

Assemble everything you need to carry: brushes, the palette, bottles of linseed oil and turpentine, a bit of rag, a small outdoor palette, a small sketching canvas, a few sticks of charcoal if you use it for underdrawing, pencils and, of course, tubes of paint.

Arrange all these on a piece of paper. The final dimensions of the box will be conditioned by what equipment you want to take; the length, for example, should obviously be sufficient to carry the longest brush you use. The depth is likely to be determined by the bottles of oil, or the number of large tubes of paint you like to carry, as well as by the option of putting canvases or a palette in the lid.

Division in the box can be arranged to suit yourself, making areas for brushes, tubes (either randomly or in sequential order), bottles of oil and turpentine, palette knives, sticks of charcoal and rags. The separators can be permanent or movable.

You can also subdivide some of the areas – for example, bringing dirty brushes home can be a nuisance; a little slotted panel keeps the clean and used brushes separate.

$16 \times 12 \times 3$ inches ($40.5 \times 30.5 \times 7.5$ cm) is a good basic proportion, although if you want to carry three or four extra canvases you will have to increase the depth to 5 inches (13 cm).

Materials for box $16 \times 12 \times 3$ inches ($40.5 \times 30.5 \times 7.5$ cm)

From $\frac{3}{16}$ inch (5 mm) plywood:
2 pieces 12×16 inches (30.5×40.5 cm)
From whitewood timber or, for additional strength and attractive finish, mahogany, beech or oak, $\frac{1}{2}$ inch (12 mm) thick:
2 lengths 16×2 inches (40.5×5 cm)
2 lengths 16×1 inches (40.5×2.5 cm)
2 lengths 11×2 inches (28×5 cm)
2 lengths 11×1 inches (28×2.5 cm)
2 hinges, $\frac{1}{2} \times 1\frac{1}{2}$ inch (12×38 mm) with their appropriate screws
2 catches
1 D-handle big enough to fit your hand – 4 inches (10 cm) at least. You can buy D-handles ready-made in almost any material, but it should be sturdy and heavy enough to hold a fully loaded box; wrought iron is attractive but not comfortable for carrying long distances. Chrome or steel is probably best, or shaped leather if you are really looking for elegance. Leather is so strong, in fact, that I had my handle made out of a simple strip of good pigskin, screwed down at each end, and it has lasted five years.

For a removable strut to hold the lid open:
$2 \times \frac{3}{4}$ inch (19 mm) round-headed screws
1 strip of $\frac{3}{16}$ inch (5 mm) plywood, 12×1 inches (30.5×2.5 cm)
Interior separators:
2 lengths $15\frac{1}{4} \times 2 \times \frac{3}{16}$ inches (38 cm $\times$ 5 cm $\times$ 5 mm) plywood
For a portable palette to go inside the box:
$14\frac{7}{8} \times 10\frac{7}{8} \times \frac{3}{16}$ inches (37.5 cm $\times$ 27.5 cm $\times$ 5 mm) plywood
Clear varnish, French polish or white knotting varnish, or paint for finishing
4 large upholstery tacks

Tools

Tenon saw
Small hammer
Chisel
Screwdriver
PVA wood glue
½ inch (12 mm) and 1 inch (25 mm) panel pins
Sandpaper
Note: If you are going to leave the box in wood finish, consider spending a little extra on wood-grain ply.

Assembly

Decide on the position of the separators. The diagram shows two compartments of 2½ inches (63 mm) each, leaving a larger compartment for tubes of paint.

On the 11 × 2 inch (28 × 5 cm) pieces of timber, measure up for the dividers and cut 2 grooves ⅛ inch (3 mm) deep and ³⁄₁₆ inch (5 mm) wide. Obviously this can't be done once you've assembled the box, so be sure to do this first.

Glue the bottom of the box together, putting the 11 × 2 inch (28 × 5 cm) timber at the sides

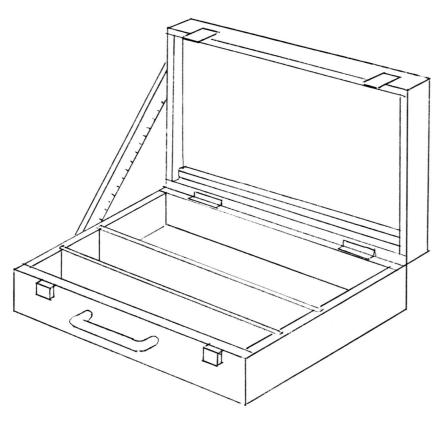

and the 16 × 2 inch (40.5 × 5 cm) timber at the front and back of one sheet of plywood. Make sure the separator grooves are opposite each other.

Turn the box over before the glue has set hard and pin together with 1 inch (25 mm) panel pins.

Put the 11 × 1 inch (28 × 2.5 cm) and the 16 × 1 inch (40.5 × 2.5 cm) timber on top of the second sheet of plywood in the same way, glueing and panel pinning together.

Glue the two ³⁄₁₆ inch (5 mm) strips of timber into the lid; this will let the palette be stored paint side to the lid, so that you can take it home still wet to clean it later.

Chisel out places for hinges. Sandpaper the outside and varnish inside and outside, or paint outside if desired. I use marine varnish, which is very strong. Alternatively, you can stain it mahogany or walnut for extra elegance. There are many new painted finishes which are very interesting – a hammered metallic finish in silver or black would make an eye-catching piece.

Fix hinges, handle and catches in place. The handle should be in the middle of the whole box, not just the base, or it will be unbalanced when you carry it.

I put the brass upholstery tacks on the bottom of the box so it clears the hinges and stands upright like a small suitcase; you can also use rubber feet, or just large round-headed screws.

To hold the strut in place when you want to keep the lid open, screw in the two round-headed screws as shown in the diagram.

Cut the notches in the strut as shown. A nice touch is to add measurements on the strut so you can use it as a convenient ruler when you need to mark up a canvas.

Make the palette by cutting a thumbhole as shown; sandpaper it and coat it with French polish, white knotting varnish or shellac. Ordinary varnish is not enough – the oil paint will bleed through and it will be impossible to clean.

2. Anatomy

Everyone has first-hand experience of anatomy; we inhabit the structures of our body, and come to the subject with vivid knowledge of what we can do and feel, even if we may not yet know why or how. Nevertheless, your representations of the human figure will benefit from a better appreciation of how the body operates. Although a knowledge of anatomy is a very useful aid to drawing, it is as well to remember that it doesn't necessarily teach you to draw any better until you can relate what you have learned to the art of drawing and painting.

The study of anatomy can be taken to quite remarkable lengths; for example, the early artists of the Renaissance attended secret dissections in order to see what lay beneath the skin for themselves.

If you become interested in the idea of anatomy for its own sake, perhaps some inquiries at the local medical school would be appropriate!

Otherwise, there are now many concise books specifically aimed at the artist who needs a particular kind of anatomical information, and those should be sufficient for your needs.

Here are a few pointers to the kind of exercise which will help you get started and show you how an acquaintence with anatomy can be of use.

Looking at a human body

Although what we see when we look at a body is skin, hair and so on, this is all just an outer covering of a frame made of bone, muscle, nerves, fat, flesh and water.

The bones make up the skeleton, which is held together with connective tissue, tendons and muscles; all are controlled by the brain through its many kinds of nerve centres. The brain of course also acts as a databank of information about everything to do with the way we breathe, move, see, think, listen, touch, smell and speak.

In theory, we could draw exactly what we see of the human body and it would be absolutely accurate. In practice we look for what we expect, and so an understanding of what is happening underneath the skin will enable us to see more clearly and precisely.

Equipment

Charcoal
Pencils
Drawing paper; a good, thick pad

First day

It's very seldom that copying is suggested as the only way to learn, but skeletal structure, like mathematical 'times tables', just has to be memorized.

Begin with the skeleton and how it is put together. Copy these drawings three or four times, writing in the names of the bones as well.

As you redraw the skeleton over and over again, look at the proportions of each part, both in itself and in relation to the other parts. For example, the skull is approximately a seventh of the height of the whole figure.

The rib cage is much wider than people usually suppose – in a skeleton, it can be seen to come out quite dramatically from the line of the spinal cord. The forearms are longer than

the upper arm – a common mistake in figure drawing is to make them shorter.

The leg proportions are reversed – the upper thigh bone is longer than the lower leg.

The wrists come down to the top of the femur, the hands below that. Another common mistake is to make the hands hang either abnormally long or abnormally short.

There are surprisingly few easily discernible differences in male and female skeletons; the pelvis is very slightly tilted in the female, the shoulder connections are slightly different, but that is all, except for the generally smaller size.

At the end of the day, draw the skeleton from memory without looking at the diagram, and see how near you approximated to the original.

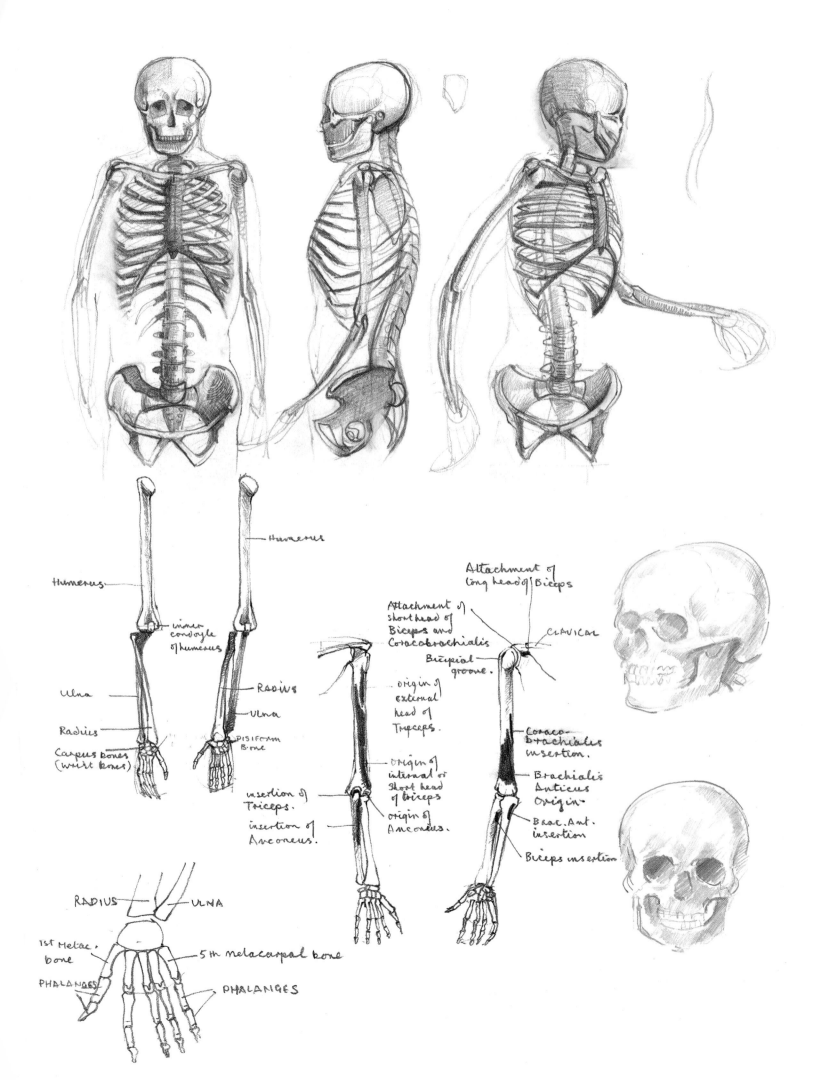

Humerus

Humerus

inner condyle of humerus

Ulna

RADIUS

ULNA

Radius

PISIFORM Bone

Carpus bones (wrist bones)

insertion of Triceps.

insertion of Anconeus.

origin of external head of Triceps.

origin of internal or Short head of biceps

origin of Anconeus.

Attachment of Long head of Biceps

Attachment of short head of Biceps and Coracobrachialis

Bicipital groove.

CLAVICAL

Coraco-brachialis insertion.

Brachialis Anticus Origin.

Brac. Ant. insertion

Biceps insertion

RADIUS

ULNA

1st Metac. bone

PHALANGES

5th metacarpal bone

PHALANGES

Second day

Here is the same skeleton covered in muscles. Repeat the exercise of drawing and redrawing the muscles, tracing how they are pulled into a few points; under the arm, at the top of the legs, at the wrists, at the neck.

The differences between the male and female body are clearer now, with men having larger shoulder development.

Again, at the end of the day, try to draw the muscle covering without looking at the original drawing.

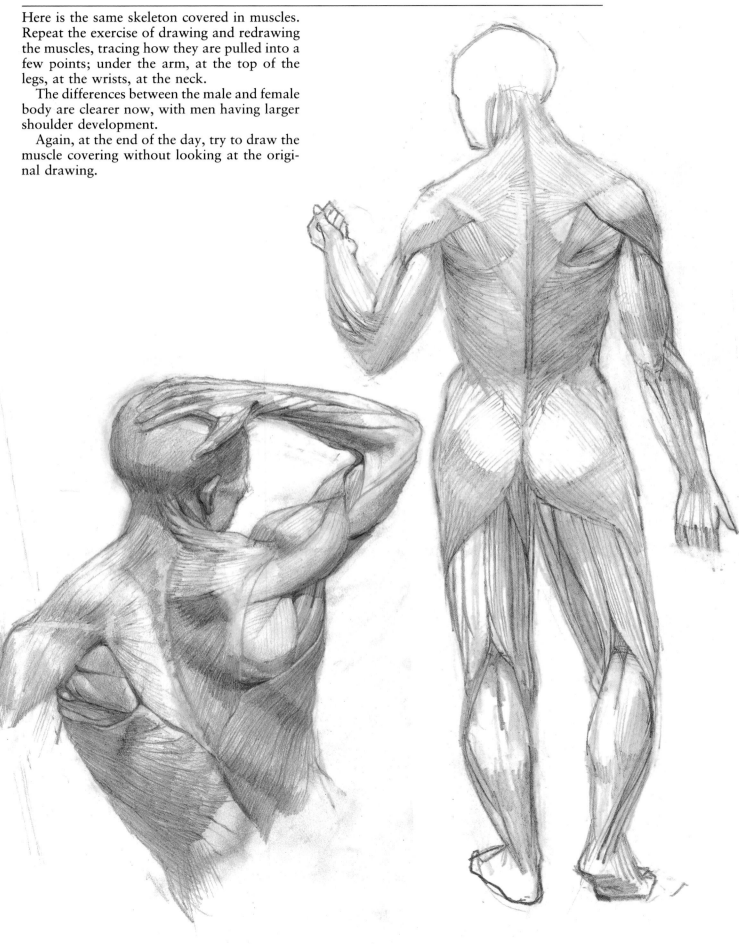

Third day

Hands and feet are without a doubt the most difficult areas for a painter – complex bone and muscle structure means that they have subtle proportions and movements which are very hard to record accurately until you have spent considerable time in observation and drawing.

Here are the skeletal structures of the left and right feet. Copy them both over and over again; we are not symmetrical images, and in human beings the two sides are often very different.

Then practise drawing your feet, and fitting the skeletal structure inside them. This is one area in which you can use your own body as a convenient model.

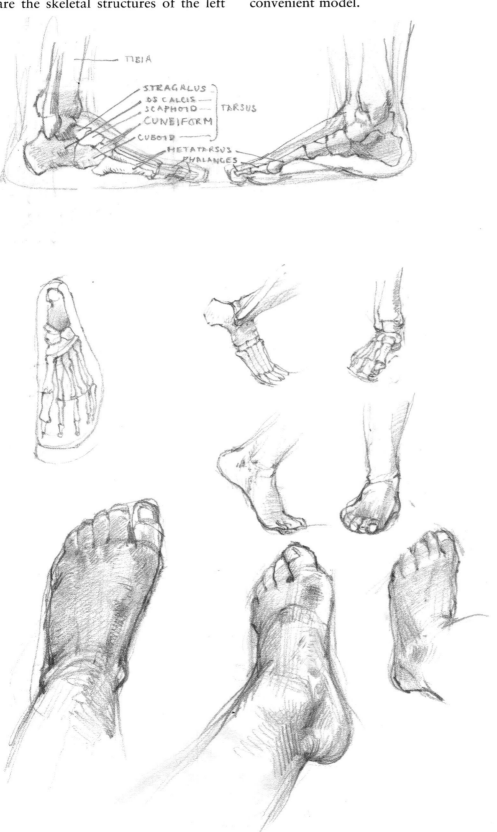

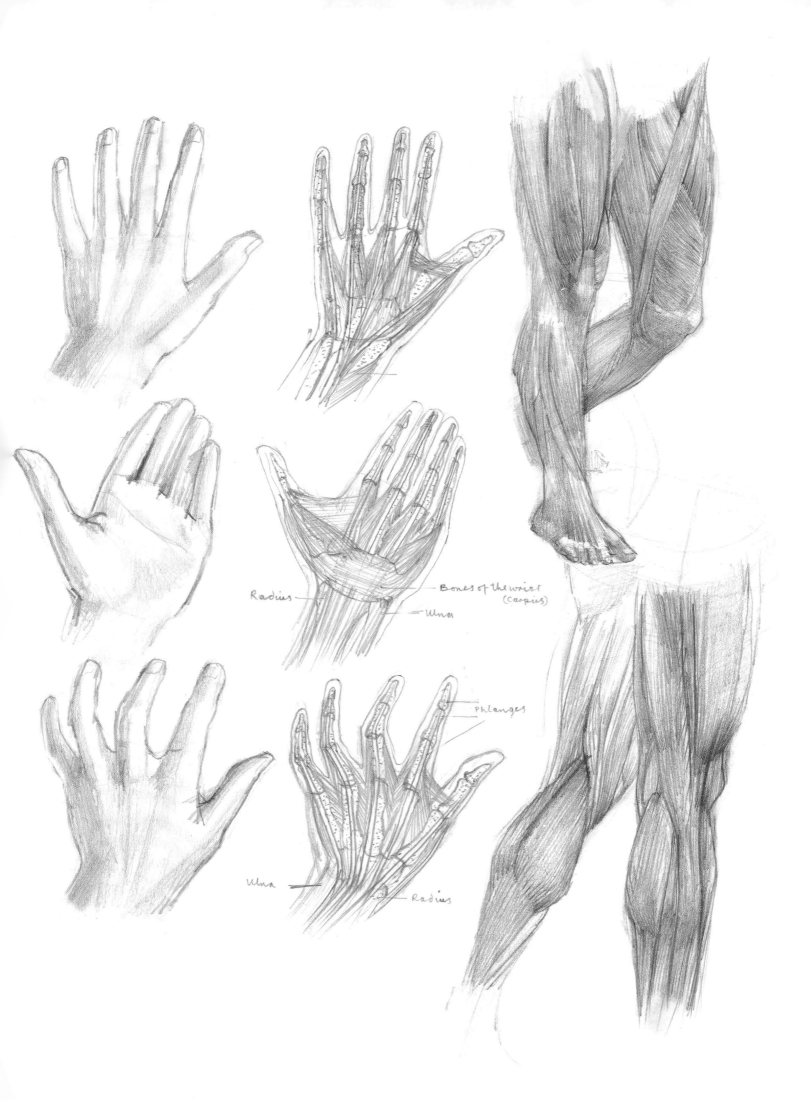

Radius

Bones of the wrist
(carpus)

Ulna

Phalanges

Ulna

Radius

Fourth day onwards

For the last part of this project you will need a model. A life class model is ideal but is not absolutely necessary as long as you can see muscles and bone structure, so a fellow artist, someone in the family or a friend or neighbour in a swim suit will do nicely.

You can draw yourself, but it is very difficult to catch an accurate view of your back without a set of mirrors, or to watch your arms and legs moving. Hands and feet are easier.

Try to draw at least six or seven poses a day. After you finish a quick sketch from life, try to draw in the skeletal outline underneath the skin to check on your ability to understand what is going on there.

Keep the model flexible and relaxed and change the angle of the joints, moving a knee or an elbow each time.

On the last day, go out and try some quick sketches of people as they walk by you, or go to a sporting event of some kind to catch glimpses of people in really extended poses. By this time your new skills in understanding the body should be a real aid to making even those quick sketches more realistic and lively.

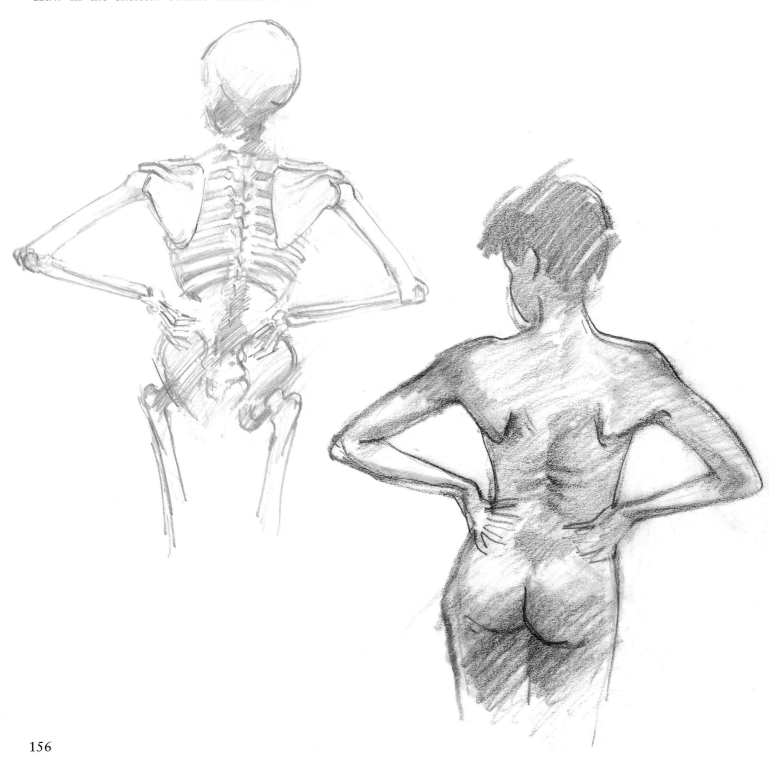

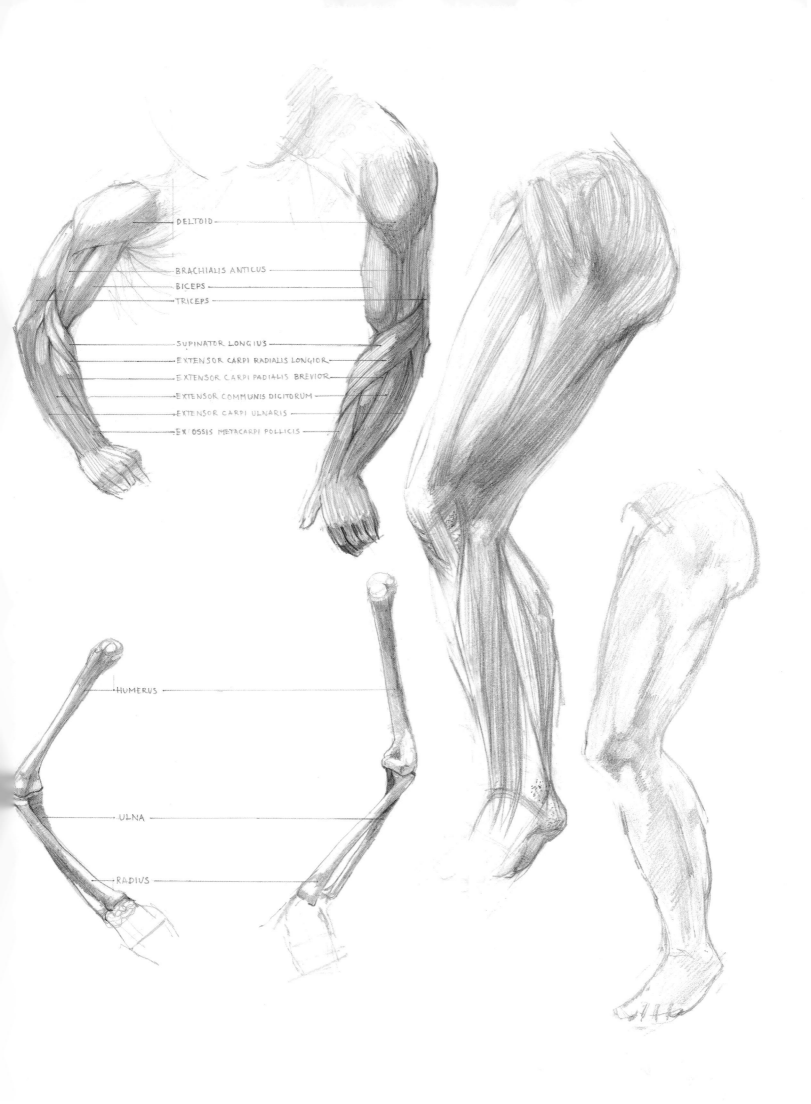

DELTOID

BRACHIALIS ANTICUS
BICEPS
TRICEPS

SUPINATOR LONGIUS
EXTENSOR CARPI RADIALIS LONGIOR
EXTENSOR CARPI RADIALIS BREVIOR
EXTENSOR COMMUNIS DIGITORUM
EXTENSOR CARPI ULNARIS
EX OSSIS METACARPI POLLICIS

HUMERUS

ULNA

RADIUS

3. Weather: studies in tone

Here is a real challenge; learning to look so carefully at the changing light and shadows that even in black and white you are able to show the effect of the weather throughout the year.

To spend long periods of time at one place, every day for a week, you have to choose somewhere which is open to the sky and the changing light, but near enough to civilization to provide you with shelter and sustenance if needed.

This is one occasion when you don't want a stretch of brilliant and cloudless weather, as this means the sky will not change dramatically from day to day.

Equipment

> Watercolour or ink in your chosen colour
> No 4 and 6 watercolour brushes in round sables
> No 8 hog hair oil brush
> Sketchbook or textured watercolour paper

Work in broad washes, using the large sable or the hog hair brush to give you the overall sky, adding detail only with darker washes and a few lines with the smaller of the brushes. You can use the darker colours after the first wash is dry, or put wet on wet to achieve the blurry effects of stormy formless clouds or the hazy colour of late afternoon. You can continue to use dry brush effects over the forms to suggest broken shadows.

Give yourself a schedule and stick to it. Do a sketch every day at noon and at 9 a.m. or 4 p.m. Make your drawing from the same place each time, looking at the same objects. Mark the hour and date in the corner of the sketch.

Don't keep looking at your earlier paintings; as you finish each one put it away, or your mind will see things that you saw the day before rather than what is in front of you now.

At the end of the project you can look at the whole series. Pin them all up together and you have a week of skyscapes.

Do the same at least once every season throughout the year, alternating colour and black and white if you like, until you are able to capture the particular moment and the effect of the weather no matter what the time of day or the season.

Somewhere in town where you can sketch every day at the same time is quite a good idea; shifting shadows will certainly be quite dramatic if there are buildings in view.

At a pinch, even a large garden will do as long as there are trees or ornaments which will give you changing shapes as the hours pass.

Go out with an empty sketchbook – you want at least ten pictures in ink and wash. Not being able to use colour is a plus – the discipline of working only in tone concentrates the mind wonderfully. Black is the usual wash used in tonal paintings, but you can use sepia, brown or, indeed, any one colour.

4. Papermaking

The earliest paper, papyrus, was made from split and flattened reeds. Modern paper is also made from vegetable matter, usually wood pulp, but the best paper for artists is made from well-washed 100 per cent cotton rag, also called cotton waste. There are other materials which are used occasionally, such as Manilla (grass) which is extremely strong but never becomes white.

Paper relies for its quality on the length of the vegetable fibre (cotton is very long, cheap wood pulp very short) and on the size, or starch, used to make it stiff and improve its writing surface; a piece of blotting paper has almost no size, cartridge paper more, and so on.

Flicking your fingernail against a piece of paper will tell you at once how much size the sheet has on its surface; a dull plop from kitchen paper, for example, will indicate no size at all, while the crisp sound from a good-quality book paper is unmistakable.

Kaolin also is added to papers used for printing to give a glossy finish and a lustre to the print; photographic books are often printed on heavily loaded kaolin paper, called art paper.

Many papers also have one 'top' side which is smoother than the other; a thick paper sheet is split and the two inner surfaces are used for smooth sheets, the outer for rough ones.

Making your own paper may not be something you will want to do all the time but, like many other hand-made processes, it will help to show exactly how paper is formed; understanding how the quality of paper is reached comes most easily when you can see the results of your own decisions.

Equipment

Two fine wire-mesh screens or trays
Paper scraps
Pieces of old blanket, larger than the trays

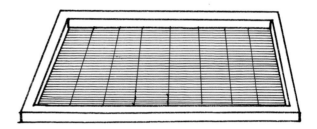

The trays can be bought purpose-made, or they can be fashioned from very fine brass mesh or even nylon curtain stretched over a wooden frame.

Ideally the frame should be double the size of sheet you want to make, as the paper will be dried by folding it across a line; when the fold is cut away you will have two flat sheets. However, if the frames are very large they may be cumbersome to use and store so, unless you have reasonable space, keep to smaller sheets for your experiments.

You can begin with old bits of clean drawing paper, scraps, offcuts from a printing house, tissues, blotting paper, etc. If you mix the colours you may get a kind of grey effect, and if you use printed papers some typeface may still appear in the finished product.

After you have tried making a simple paper sheet, why not enjoy the variety that hand-made processes offer and add a few leaves, ferns, flowers and any other unusual scraps. The colour and texture will produce some very pleasing effects.

Soak the scraps in water until they become pulp. This will take several days. Stir occasionally into a kind of porridge; the mixture should have the texture of a glutinous paste. For this week's project you should make up around 2 gallons (9 litres) of pulp – it can be left to soak in ordinary plastic buckets, one perhaps with coloured papers, and others with newspaper, leaves, flowers, etc.

The next step is to pour out the pulp into the tray to make one sheet. You will have to use a certain amount of trial and error because so much depends on exactly what you put into the pulp, how warm or cold the temperature of the room is, how much water you added and so on.

Take a little of the mixture and swirl it around on the tray as if you were coating a frying pan with pancake batter. Give it a shake; the result should be a fairly thin, even layer. If there is not enough water you'll get a stiff dough; if it is too liquid it will all run through the mesh, leaving a kind of tissue. As each kind of paper used for the pulp has its own absorbency rate, you will simply have to try it and see.

It is better to start with as little water as possible and add more, rather than begin with too much.

A pulp of old paper will probably have enough size in it already to hold the sheet together. If your first experiments fall apart, then you need to add some size. Start with roughly 1 gallon (4.5 litres) of pulp to a tablespoon of size dissolved in a cupful of warm water. You can add more as needed.

When you have what seems to be the right consistency, put a good cupful of pulp on to the tray, swirl to spread it out and shake the tray sharply to make a flat layer. Let it sit for a few minutes to set in place, then turn the tray over on to a piece of blanket to absorb any excess moisture.

If you are making several sheets at once you can pile them up, alternating them with blanket pieces. Top with a board and a heavy weight and leave until most of the water has been absorbed into the blankets.

Finish by folding the sheets across a line and letting them hang in a warm, dry room until they are completely dry and ready to use.

During the week

Once you have the knack of judging the right consistency for the pulp and the right amount to swirl into the tray, you can start experimenting with different-coloured pulps, added textures and so on. You can also create texture on the surface by scattering it with leaves and flowers after the sheet is turned out and left to dry.

Put your own watermark on to your paper by taking some fine fuse wire and weaving it in and out of the heavy wires of the base screen into a little pattern – your initials, perhaps, or a design which becomes your own mark. The pulp is forced into the wire patterns when you pour it on to the tray. This only works well with plain, fine-textured paper; if you have added all kinds of material to the pulp the design is not likely to show up.

For very smooth paper, use a fine pulp mixture and after it has been taken out of the blanket pile (and before it has dried completely) flip it on to a flat Formica surface and iron it with a dry iron to give a very smooth, hot press surface on one or both sides. It will not need any further drying.

Alternative papers

Here are some of the additions which you can add to the pulp:
Newsprint, white or pink (remember the financial papers!); cartons from commercial packaging, in this case a carton from a major hamburger chain; paper tissues of various colours; fresh flowers (forsythia in the photograph) skeletonized leaves, which have been eaten away by grubs, far more effective in the finished paper than whole leaves; dried flowers and leaves, in any combination of textures and colours; a few scrap paper bits, both from ordinary cards and whatever is left from other hand-made paper sheets; blotting papers; used envelopes; brown wrapping paper.

5. Texture and detail in still life

When you work on something as palpable and recognizable as a still-life painting, it becomes doubly important to be able to translate what you see accurately on to the canvas.

You have to work with two conflicting perceptions: the knowledge of a very familiar object – a bowl of grapes, an apple – which enables your brain to identify a number of small oval shapes in a bunch, a rounded red and green sphere; and the awareness of what you are actually seeing – perhaps only a smudge or two of dark purple and a half-moon shape of bright red.

Still-life painting, at its best, is a re-creation of the reality using only subtle hints; getting the texture and detail right is much more important than carefully reproducing every piece of fruit in the bowl.

Left and right, below. Using different backgrounds. It can change the richness of the painting immediately.

Focus and perspective

Aerial perspective is used extensively in Dutch still-life painting. The colour tones grow paler with distance from the viewer, even though the distance is in fact only a matter of inches to the back of the table rather than the miles depicted in a landscape. The focus also changes so that the apples shown here in the foreground have an intensity of colour and a sharpness of detail which rapidly decrease as the images recede.

Texture

The paint itself can represent texture; for example, dots of pigment can act as the seeds of a fig.

Texture can also be created by dabbing the paint so that it gives the impression of a rough surface, like an avocado skin.

Colour blending is another tool with which to achieve a particular texture. This involves working with two or three colours blended together to give a soft, mutating colour range – a technique which is particularly successful for creating the illusion of a fuzzy, rounded peach.

The final touches bring life to the painting; pick out a peach which is perhaps more dominant than the others, or a leaf which glows more deeply and adds depth to the composition. You have to play around with the truth and make that peach just a little larger, more brilliant in colour, than you actually see it, the leaf a little glossier, a little greener.

Tricks of the trade

Still-life painting, especially as refined by the Dutch and Flemish masters, is one of the most attractive of the traditional styles. Their ability to capture the various textures of fruit, feather and flora relied on accurate perception and concentration on every tiny detail of colour, light and shadow.

If you want to explore that tradition yourself, here are a few hints to get you started.

This is not a project which should be rushed. Set up your original composition where the light won't change over the week – perhaps you can use electric light, although it should be heavily shaded and angled from the side – and choose fruit in good condition so that it doesn't deteriorate over the week. Without moving the contents, transfer the basket of fruit to a refrigerator when you are not working.

After a few preliminary drawings, the first part of the project should consist of getting the overall subject down on the canvas using rich, dark oil colours, put on in thin layers and glazed over and over again.

Use soft brushes and pigment with a great deal of fluidity, mixing a quarter of pure turpentine to three-quarters of raw linseed oil and very little pigment.

You will never achieve the most realistic representation of individual fruits if you simply paint them the colour that they are.

To keep the luminous sheen on the skins: If you are painting a lemon or a pale peach, try painting it white first, letting it dry completely, and then washing it over with a touch of pale cadmium yellow added to a brushful of linseed oil. Let it dry again. Add another glaze of linseed oil, this time with a touch of raw sienna for the shadows, and let it dry for the final time.

Use the reverse colour spectrum for painting a bunch of black grapes or a fig. Begin with black underpainting. When it is completely dry, glaze over with a brushful of linseed oil mixed with a touch of purple and a tiny touch of white to make the purple slightly cloudy and give you an opalescent sheen. Instead of adding shadows you can wipe off the purple where the shadows are, leaving the black

showing through, and adding just a touch more purple for the highlights.

In the same painting, a banana might need a single stroke of yellow with a palette knife. Its ripe, brown speckling can be achieved either by letting the yellow dry and then painting on the dots carefully, stippling first and then wiping or blurring the edges a little, or by working wet brown into the wet yellow paint, or, alternatively, by adding spots of glaze with raw umber.

The important point is to vary your technique wherever necessary to give the right effect for that particular part of the painting; all the techniques might even be employed on the same banana to get the right effects.

Detail

You have to use paint to imitate the reality, to suggest and imply rather than to merely copy. After all, if you are painting a piece of fabric you don't paint every thread, but you aim for something that looks as if you have!

This tablecloth has a flat, dull surface so you begin with the flat colour of the fabric itself. Then you need to put another layer on with short cross-strokes which suggest the warp and weft of the fabric. Work over the pattern by dry brushing in a little white to catch the light here and there as the cloth would. Where the shadow falls, and you have darkened the colour range, remember to keep the edge of the shadow slightly broken, as it would be in reality where the light catches a rough surface.

If the fabric were glazed cotton or silk you would treat it like glass; crisp edges, a glazed surface and highlights defined by straight, clean edges.

Achieving detail doesn't necessarily mean putting in, say, every tiny imperfection in the skin of a pomegranate. Although many great still-life masterpieces look as if every detail is on the canvas, if you go in very close, you'll see it is not so, the artists knew that often the sum of the parts does not add up to a whole.

Knowing which details and textures to use and which to leave out is the special skill of creating vivid still lifes.

*Right and below;
traditional examples
are a great help in
understanding how
texture and detail help
in creating the final
impression. Studying
the great Dutch
masters repays every
minute in improving
your techniques.*

6. Problems of the larger composition

The problems of working on a larger scale than normal are similar to those of catering for a very large party; your equipment and techniques have to be different from the start, and you cannot simply double or treble the ingredients – the proportions change, too.

There are two concepts to consider: first, the different requirements when working on a grand scale, and second, the transforming of a small sketch or painting into a larger one.

Changing the scale of a painting means losing a lot of preconceptions. The painting itself will be seen from yards, rather than feet, away, and almost certainly at a different eye-level, too. The viewer will simply not be able to take in small, delicate details, so all the formerly fine touches have to be transmuted into grand flourishes.

Working close up is impossible; it's a good idea to practise painting at arm's length so you can keep some sort of focus on what you are doing. Moving back and forth in front of a large painting can be physically exhausting; if you concentrate on doing a small bit and then keep walking back to look at it your memory and vision have to constantly re-focus. Some artists tie the brush or charcoal on to a long light stick; a bamboo cane of about 3 ft (91 cm), split at the end to enclose the brush, is a remarkably simple solution and gives you double your arm's length.

Every part of the picture is obviously going to be larger. On a normal-sized canvas, the viewer's eye skims over a brush or two of plain colour in the foreground. In a large painting these two brushstrokes become eight or nine, and that amount of flat colour can be very dull and boring. You have to find different techniques for filling the area with modelling and shadows, perhaps a slight pattern or texture, something which will satisfy the eye without intruding into the main picture.

A really large area of any one colour or tone can be very dominant, its emphasis out of proportion to the actual space taken up.

Contrasts in tone and colour actually have to be less the larger the work. Black and white in a small picture are acceptable; on a large scale they are overpowering, and a series of closely toned greys and whites is preferable.

Here and on the following spread, details from a large mural featuring a town harbour and its fishing trade.

Scaling up a small picture

You will need to work in the same proportion as the original. Make two grids on paper, copy the lines in each small square on to the larger square, and you have a cartoon, or sketched outline, to work from.

The sketch, even at the right size, should not be used for the finished painting without adjustment. Just consider one point; on a large wall painting, the base of the original picture, which probably hung at eye level, will move down to floor level, and it will be viewed from above. Details which you formerly saw straight ahead of you are now well below eye-level, so the perspective has to change.

The size of figures is also important. Larger-than-lifesize figures are generally uncomfortable to look at, unless the painting is hung so high up that the figures look human after all.

Project

Plan a large mural of your neighbourhood. Choose an area that you know well and enjoy looking at – perhaps a small street of shops, a church and its churchyard with facing houses, or a terrace of small homes.

Think about making it into a narrative – perhaps depicting a bad storm, a local wedding, a carnival or a fair.

Traditional wall painting with tempera on plaster is a problem nowadays – it's better to use something more portable. A roll of lining paper or photographic background paper can be taped securely to the wall itself and work in quick-drying acrylic.

Begin by making a lot of small sketches on the spot, taking photographs and looking up some local history in the library or town hall.

It might be fun to add some local characters as well. So it can become a community affair.

Make a small sketch of the chosen scene, with all the characters in place; it should be as finished as possible, so you will be able to scale

Fraserborough Mural for TOTAL reception hall St. Fergus.
Size 8×5 feet framed, painted on canvas with ALKYD

Scene shows working-fishermen and ancillary helpers — in
the harbour. Centrepiece the unloading and preparing
-boxing fish for ~~market~~ distribution, in and about the
Fishmarket. preparing boats for fishing — nets — ice
repairs, fixing lights etc. Boats in harbour. spectators.
General ~~composition~~ view — shows reflections, sky
gulls. Rigging. boxes. nets drying on quayside.
the tower.

Red Beak

Black Headed
Gull
Summer

Dk red claws

BOATS IN HARBOUR

Fish Market

Seiner trawler 70ft.   Seiner fishing practised from Iceland
                        white fish. Cod. haddock

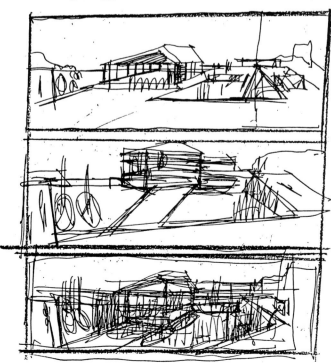

boat
shelter   wheelhouse

typical Seiner trawler shape this one however is new + smaller than
the old kind

Seiner
winch

Seine Rope drums (Hydraulically moved)
vary somewhat with each trawler.   Alfred Daniels '78

it up as suggested above, remembering to adjust the proportions and perspective as you work.

After scaling up, start with a full-size drawing in charcoal. Put in everything you want to include, keeping the lines light enough to be blown or brushed off later. This should give you a good idea if the composition is working, and you can check the scale and perspective before you begin to paint.

Block in the main areas and keep working all over the picture. Do not concentrate on one small patch for a long time, or you will end up with six or seven small pictures that simply bleed into each other. Learning to see the whole as one composition is one of the most important points of working on a grand scale.

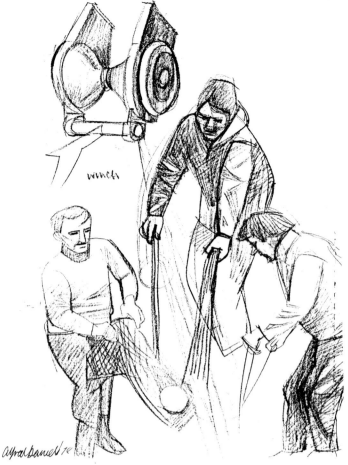

7. Nature sketch album

Looking for nature

Finding places and subjects to draw in the country can sometimes be much harder than it sounds. At first the idea of wonderful wide open spaces seems to expand into an artist's paradise, but practical experience around cultivated farmland will show how many obstacles there are; roads lined with trees or hedges make it impossible to see, the few places where you can stop are often tractor gates for the farmer, and consequently deep in muddy ruts and cowpats, while barbed wire fences everywhere stop you from trespassing, and also from finding the perfect viewpoint.

Woodlands are more accessible, but although trees crowded around your easel can inspire some unusual angles, there is no horizon, little change in the light, and often a general air of quiet gloom.

Years ago, I realized that there were two kinds of excursions which were most fruitful for me – landscape trips lasting usually a few days or more, when I could spend time finding the right place to set up an easel, with a view that had seemed interesting to me, and where I would be able to take the car somewhere nearby with all the equipment and spend whatever time I needed to make that one painting work.

But by far the most varied and useful excursions are short sketching walks, when I make little drawings or paintings for a homemade nature album. Sometimes I can spend an afternoon in the countryside, sometimes I have no more than a brief hour at lunch for a collage of quick impressions, a leaf, a flower, or a branch, using whatever medium was to hand, convenient for the weather and the time of year.

This appreciation of how I work makes it easy to find something to do no matter where I am or how much time I have to spare, and I suggest that anyone can sort out their priorities in a similar way.

Right: as a complete contrast, try making a vivid oil sketch of a huge flower bed – no details or textures, just blobs of brilliant colours and a few stems to hold the "blossoms" in shape on the canvas.

Below: it is always important to remember how the whole plant looks; if you make a small pattern from part of a morning glory vine, as I did below, then draw the outline of the whole vine as a sketch, so you keep a sense of proportion.

Far left: try to capture more than the appearance of a plant. This little daisy turned its head to the sun, all through the day. I came back every two hours to draw it from the same position.

Left: another daisy, this time as a serious "portrait" isolating the flowerhead against a washed-in background of turquoise blue to let the full impact of white and yellow speak for itself.

Above: yet another approach, each leaf studied in the most minute detail so that the individual textures and features of each plant – even each leaf – are delineated. A sharp, hard pencil or pen and ink are the best mediums; charcoal would be far too broad, and even a very tiny watercolour brush might tend to be uneven.

If you can learn to look around with an enquiring eye, there are miniature miracles of nature everywhere. The smallest strip of grass can contain a lovely clump of flowering grasses, a crevice in derelict house often serves as home to a flowering poppy or a young tree. Out in the wilderness, I've seen the incredible veining of a fallen branch and a mushroom, the strange pattern of flaking bark, a simple daisy turning in the sun, or a rich kaleidoscope of colours shining from a flower bed conveniently near a comfortable park bench.

Pens, pencils, a box of pastels or thin charcoal sticks and those very small watercolour boxes which hold 9 tiny pans are all convenient to use. An equally miniature vial of water will provide enough for quite a few sketches, and a bit of paper tissue will keep brush and paper clean.

Try and keep a sketchbook in your pocket or briefcase for the odd glimpse of a flower or leaf. When you have a little more time, you can use larger sheets of paper and even an easel if necessary. This can be very convenient when you want to work in great detail, hard to do if you are crouching over a tiny 6″ viola. Practice with something that you can pick without any chance of uprooting an endangered flower or plant – a head of wheat, or a few leaves from common or garden trees. Pin the leaf to the top of the paper, and you can work for an hour or more without straining your eyes or your neck muscles!

Look at different ways of portraying your subjects, too. Because you are working with nature's plants there is no reason to imagine they must all be botanical studies.

Patterns and design

These are found in the visual pictures that plants make, as well as in the structure of the plants themselves. An example of the first is the section of a morning glory vine on the previous page. When you look at the plant originally, you may see nothing but a complete tangle of leaves and flowers. But with care and attention, your eye can carve out a self-contained section by working around an outline that seems to enclose an interesting pattern. Extra leaves and petals that fall outside your chosen area can either be ignored, or utilized to make a broken, perhaps more interesting edge.

I have built up quite a collection of scrapbooks, dating back to my student days filled with notes and brief colour charts, marking the place and the time of the year, and anything special I noted at the time about the subject, the atmosphere, the colours or the place.

When I am find myself at a standstill on a large landscape, worried about some aspect of the overall effect, or unhappy about the detail, then I need to take a break, and leafing through the albums can spark off a whole new approach, so that I can return to the easel with a fresh eye.

Here are a few pages from my own sketching album which show how much can be done with just pen and ink, a few felt-tip colours, and a tube each of green and white oil paint.

You can play around with outlines as I did, left, on the sketch of ragwort, with shading and monocolour effects shown on the two other sketches below, and even with a tube or two of paint to make the simplest representation of a tall sprig of cow parsley, on the right.

Everyone always assumes that oil paintings have to be thickly covered, elaborate affairs, but here just green was used in a wash for the background and in thin lines for the plant – the only other note of colour was a few touches of white for the flower heads.

Even if you use different surfaces and media for your sketches, try and keep them the same size, so that you can trim the separate pieces and keep them together in a folder.

8. Reflections

The double image is a powerful theme in painting and also in films, where a fleeting glimpse of a familiar face reflected in a car window or of the Eiffel tower reflected in a revolving door set the atmosphere and the scene more vividly than a long sequence of deliberate 'frontal' views.

Another obvious enjoyment in painting reflections is the chance it gives to see an image twice – the austere house on the canal becomes a wavering, softened image in the water, a white swan on a calm lake is doubled in beauty and makes for a surreal, upside-down world.

Most classical reflections in art are seen in water. Canaletto's views of Venice are probably the most famous of the genre; Cotman and Constable both used reflections of trees and bridges to suggest calm and tranquillity. Nearer our own time, Monet's Waterlily series, based on his own pool at Giverny, must be nearly as well known, while Renoir and Manet used the Seine to marvellous effect,

with every colour from black to opalescent blue and purple reflected in its waters.

Don't imagine that you need a lake or grand canal to give you the same effect; try a single flower in a glass, standing behind a shallow bowl of water.

Look for puddles when it rains, and the reflections of brilliant shop lights on the darkened pavement, especially at night.

However, there are other reflections to look for; mirrors can give an amusing chance to show yourself in an apparently objective painting – Velásquez showed how delightful the effect can be in his portrait of the Spanish Infanta – and many of the Dutch paintings also contain reflections from this useful source.

Also of interest are the strange effects of reflections in windows; this photograph, made while taking pictures for an early project, seems at first glance to show a garden urn rising out of a clump of bushes – the perfect subject for a surreal painting.

Here are a few examples of what to look for; a drawing of a bridge in Venice, a model posing in front of a mirror, a boat on the river.

Make a whole sketchbook full of reflections, not forgetting the puddles on a rainy night; remember that the reflection is not only another viewpoint, but often, with the light refracted, it is blurred a little, adding a ghost-like quality to some paintings, a feeling of depth to others.

Look at the colour values and how they change as well as the outlines.

When you are working with oil, you can paint the reflection in thin straight lines, and then blur them by running across the lines with a dry brush. However, when using water-colour, you need to put in the broken lines directly as you work.

9. A studio portrait

Portrait painting is a craft on its own. Figure studies, the nearest relative, show how to represent a body with a bone structure, weight, substance and muscles. That ability to capture the look of a living human being is not shared by every artist, and there are many well-known painters who are careful to avoid using realistic likenesses of figures in their compositions. Painting or drawing a likeness of someone is an additional skill, however. It is not only a living face, but that particular face, not just a smile but that special smile, that must be captured.

For some artists portraits come easily, whether they be a richly detailed representation of shape, colour and form or a light, glancing sketch which none the less manages to capture the tilt of the head, the wave of hair on the brow.

For others, a portrait requires a great deal of hard work and endless sittings, and still the result may be disappointing.

Nevertheless, it is such an exciting subject that it should be tried seriously at least once. In the history of art there are few painters who didn't essay a portrait now and then, and there are many who painted almost nothing else. There is a variety of classic approaches you should study, from the flat, primitive portrait reminiscent of the early Egyptian wall panels to the dramatic realism of court painters. Later came the romantic, glowing portraits of the Impressionists, and, in our own time, the stylized faces of contemporary art.

It should be fairly easy to find a model; most of us are quite intrigued to discover what others see in us! This project should not be a self-portrait; you know yourself too well, and it won't give you experience in capturing someone else's image on paper or canvas. The best choice is someone living conveniently nearby, who can sit for one or two short sessions every day during the week.

A friend, neighbour, or member of the family is a natural choice. To avoid any unrealistic expectations, both artist and sitter might do well to remember that there is almost always an emotional conflict between them; the sitter is trying to look like the person he or she would like to be, while the artist is looking for distinctive attributes which the sitter may never recognize in the mirror but which will turn an academic study into a lifelike portrayal. In the end, of course, the viewer is only aware of what the artist wanted to show, not what the sitter might have felt.

The greatest portraits are the product of these tensions and even if the artist is a rank amateur they still exist – so a certain amount of social chat is a good idea to create a relaxed atmosphere early on in the sittings.

You will have to decide on the approach you are going to use. Leaving aside a highly stylized picture, which would be more about the image than the person, there are two basic ways to portray a likeness.

A careful, slowly worked image with every detail in its exact place will, eventually, produce a reasonable reflection of the right colours, tones and shapes. Photo-realism is the extreme version of this approach, but you needn't go quite that far.

If you want to experiment with this technique you will need to make a grid on your canvas, the squares no more than 1 inch (2.5 cm) in size. Work through the underdrawing, the blocking out and the final details, each time painting square by square, with an occasional foray into an overall reworking to blend everything together.

The second approach is more traditional; a portrait painted in the usual way, from the first sketch to a finished painting, thoughtful and careful, but with plenty of room for expressive use of the brush and an interesting palette.

Another important choice concerns the pose. Many possibilities have opened up since the formal and rather stiff portraits of the 17th and 18th centuries, and we have become used to informal settings as well as informal poses; this can be useful in bringing in all sorts of coloured and patterned backgrounds. When someone you know well has a characteristic way of sitting, take advantage of it – that alone can be enough to make him or her instantly recognizable.

Make your first sitting a relaxed session for getting to know each other and trying to assess how you see the person. Ask yourself what would help to make the image come to life.

Use the time to make pages of preparatory drawings. Try sketching the head from different angles, against variously patterned cloths and with lights coming from one side, then the other; none of us have a symmetrical face and it is amazing how different we look when the source of light is moved. Do remember not to have the light too low, beneath the face, unless you are planning something that could be used to advertise a horror movie!

Don't ask the sitter to hold any particular pose for too long – you want as wide a choice as possible from which to make the final

Above, find a patient friend to let you try lighting faces from every direction; and see how the first, lit from below, is a disaster!

decision. Try a few bits of fabric draped over the shoulder to see the effect of different clothes.

After you look at the sketches you may decide on just a head, a head and shoulders or a three-quarter-length seated figure. Talk to the sitter about clothes; you want something comfortable for him or her to wear but interesting for you to paint; something which will bring out the colour and tones in the model's face and hair.

Set up your working space for the next day. Find somewhere you can put up your easel and the sitter's chair and leave them up for the week. Remember this is a long project, so the sitter needs to be comfortable and the room warm enough for both of you to be at ease.

Check the lighting; unless you have a north-lit studio it makes sense to use electric light. Then you can work whenever you feel like it throughout the week, and at any time convenient to you both.

10. Animals in action

The concept of movement, of capturing living creatures in action, necessitates a technique which is quite different from the thoughtful approach of cerebral planning. You need a way of recording things instantly as you see them happen.

You must develop an automatic response towards catching movement; you have only a momentary glimpse of the object and you have to put it down instantly.

This talent is something that only comes with practice, and there are three things which you have to try to learn.

You need to develop a way of remembering what you see. Those people with photographic memories are obviously at an advantage while others have to train theirs as best they can, because the image must stay in the brain longer than it takes to move by you in reality. Even if you only retain the image for two or three minutes, that will be enough to record it.

Secondly, you have to develop a drawing skill that captures that image very accurately and rapidly – in other words, you are drawing from memory, even though the memory is only a few seconds old.

Thirdly, you have to learn to stress and even exaggerate the important features of the animal so that the sense of movement is there – an outstretched paw, for example, needs to be longer, bigger, because that is the striking force of the image. Do not copy nature, but let nature itself exaggerate elements of reality to produce the truth. It is the same technique used in quick sketches of any kind – a kind of distillation of the essentials.

This is something which you can practise. If you have a dog or cat at home it is obviously an asset, but you can do the same trick by flicking your own hand, then trying to draw it.

Places to visit where you will find an excellent range of subjects include farms, zoos, race courses, horse trials, pet shows and sheepdog trials. Take along a sketchbook and use the opportunity to practise your memory and drawing skills.

Jut in case you think animal painting is a Renaissance invention, here is a detail from a tiny medieval illumination, the horse and rider with his falcon, portrayed with accuracy and a sense of humour.

Four Special Projects

1. Still life
2. People
3. Flowers
4. Distant landscape

Tom Ross

1. Still life

For almost all painters past and present, still life was the first subject they tackled. Over and over again, the simple composition of a plate, an apple and perhaps a bottle of wine marks the beginning of a lifetime's fascination with brush and paint. They have managed to create, often with very basic objects, a remarkable sense of atmosphere, of time and place and period.

Above all, the examples shown here should encourage imagination and creativity. You can begin with anything, and without colour as well. Try finding a pattern in the photograph of this group of bottles in all sizes and shapes, or see how well you can convey the feel of these domestic cooking utensils with the rough, tonal texture of stoneware.

Here are two more ideas to set you going; a very simple pot of chrysanthemums, in pen, ink, and a little blue wash makes a lovely study – the slightly raised eye level, looking down into the pot, gives an edge to what might have been a very conventional sketch.

Below is a complete contrast – a very complex painting in the most subtle tones and colourings, yet the subject is still very ordinary; a prosaic mantelpiece in a family scullery. As you look closely, jugs and bottles, washing-up brush and an old mirror gradually appear in a sequence of blues, violets and grays. Only one strange shape stands out – a sheep skull, originally a remnant from a child's interest in biology, but now used often in Fred Cuming's paintings because of its bone structure to add a memento mori to the composition, much as the Dutch masters often included symbols of death amidst their most luscious fruit and flower studies. Note how the straight line of the objects on the mantelpiece, which could have made a boring composition, has been broken up skilfully by the varying heights and shapes, the depth from front to back on the shelf, and the squared panels of the window and mirror frame above, and the inset fire and mantelpiece support below.

More examples of how you can make simple subjects exciting; lighting a plain white cup and saucer from the side shows up all the variations in tone and colour; bottles of vinegar, painted in the most delicate of watercolour washes, as delicious as their contents; opposite, black and white drawings in an unusual technique using dots instead of line, and below, a romantic setting for tea in a summer garden; the single strong touch of red as a focal point brings the whole composition together.

Working on still life paintings can be full of surprises; the pencil sketch of a potted plant, on the opposite page, was the beginning of the table-top oil painting below it. Gradually the artist included an orange, an apple, a crumpled napkin and a white block vase, but when the painting was almost finished, he decided the plant was too green, and changed it for a bowl of aurum lilies.

On the right a painting which included the favourite objects of the room's owner; a bronze head, a lovely round-backed Victorian chair, a Venetian painted glass. Since the room was full of books, the painter had the perfect background already set up!

So that we don't forget that the greatest painters in the world have also found pleasure and delight in the most ordinary subjects, this basket with vegetables, a bowl of cherries and flowers was painted in the 16th century, by Caravaggio.

2. People

Of all the subjects for the artist, human beings are surely the most complex and fascinating objects! Medieval books and manuscripts, in a tradition that lasted well into the modern world, almost always show people doing things, as actors, so to speak, in the play of life. Examples include a gatekeeper and soldier in a castellated town, two women in an Italian 18th-century kitchen, a French king on his throne, with a solemn stare suitable for majesty, while Ghengis Khan, across, is also set within a circle of adoring courtiers.

We looked at painting portraits in some of the previous projects. But this project is a good time to try and see the other side of the coin, learning to look at people rather than persons. On the following two pages there are four sketches – an old man, a rather sad woman, a young girl slumped in her chair, an arrogant young man. The emphasis is not on the individual but on their human-ness.

Finally, on pages 204 and 205, there are more elaborate examples of people as images; the old woman reading, enveloped in her chair, the romantic beauty enveloped in roses, and a modern pastiche of Godiva enveloped in hair.

3. Flowers

Looking at flowers – what could be more enjoyable! From the first time a youngster draws a daisy face, flowers play an important part in our vocabulary. Roses are red, shrinking violets, pure lilies, hot-house orchids ... the list goes on and on.

From the earliest times flower heads and leaves, and the fruits which are the ultimate result of the flowers, were used constantly as patterns on pottery and glass; there are medieval manuscripts with borders filled with flower heads, hedgerow blossoms and berries, cultivated sprays for pot pourri, single wild flowers and huge bouquets of herbal aromatics.

Illustrated flowers were drawn in paintings for their symbolism, usually religious, or their use in a coat of arms or a badge of honour – the Tudor rose is only one example.

Flowers were also part of the medicine of the time; since almost everything was based on herbs, then it was vital to know as much as possible about how each flower looked. This was the beginning of botanical illustration, and it remains today one of the most prized forms which flower painting has achieved. Original drawings and prints from the sixteenth century onwards sell for truly remarkable figures in the auction houses, and examples of how they often pictured the entire plant from seed to fruiting stem (an example can be seen below left) can be easily found reproduced in modern collections. Even in this decade there have been new 'floraligiums' which continue to explore the modern botanical style.

Of course, still life paintings often include individual flowers or arrangements of some considerable elaboration but flower studies of single individual branches or sprays are less common. Yet they can be as varied as the delicate wet on wet image of an rose on the right, or simply-painted houseplants, below.

But the fun of taking something as universal as flowers for a major project is finding them in a hundred different styles and techniques. Open your eyes and you'll find your inspiration everywhere.

Just above here is the sharply linear pen and ink design for a formal bouquet, its Victorian precision a complete antithesis to the previous examples. Then there are flowered borders, even in the smallest streets, with subjects for you to make endless drawings.

Another find-drawn pen drawing on the right creates a completely different effect, the iris stems and petals making an all-over design which could easily become a wall-paper or fabric.

And finally on the opposite page a whole host of flower patterns – in a marble carving, an embroidered sampler, even a 1930s stylized china border.

Paint them all, in as many different kinds of mediums as you can – petals in splodges of watercolours or clear linear outlines; leaves in colour or black and white, stems carefully drawn in or just suggested with a smudge. Once you begin to look for flowers, you'll see them everywhere; an album of flowers will be something to add to as long as you go on painting.

4. Distant Landscape

The artist has always had a love affair with nature of all kinds, but far and away the most satisfying subject for me is a distant landscape. Landscape of any sort, true, because somehow in laying down the soft colours of the fold of hills and the patterns of field and hedgerow, difficulties and worries are smoothed away, but distant landscapes in particular.

The feeling that I can see to the ends of the earth, a wide perspective that seems to stretch to the horizon, creates pleasure in just being there to discover such a view, and a sense of fulfilment in the painting of it. Learn to look everywhere; sometimes the inspiration comes from the briefest glimpse when I am on holiday, or an angle of a hill that I see above the streets of almost any small town in the countryside.

Other sources are paintings by artists, past and present. Before the Renaissance, rural landscapes were seldom if ever used as the

main subject, but there were usually glimpses of the Italian hills (far left, below).

Later there were prints and etchings, perhaps sometimes a little self-consciously based on 'dramatic' views, like the example below left, but surely the none the worst for that! The hoary trees and mysterious grotto can be translated into a much simplified modern oils with their dark foreground and distant sunshine on the fields, above.

Most often, though, I find there is a truly extraordinary amount of material in modern work, either realist or impressionistic. It would seem that every part of our earth has been utilized as a resource by an artist, somewhere; look at the wildly different and yet impressive possibilities on this page.

211

The paintings here reflect ways of approaching what is essentially the same subject, open fields under a cloudy sky.

Below is a simplified scene, painted for a school mural – the lines of the fields are easy, there are no threatening hills, or mysterious grottos. All the summer days will be sunny, the grain will grow and fill the distant silos, the trees will stand tall and green, and families will cook dinner in the farmhouse. The tractor is moving, but not quickly, without rushing, without pressure to finish or to be somewhere else. Never underestimate the power of happiness and optimism in your work. If looking at a scene makes you feel good, then paint it that way – the work draws strength from you, and reflects that contentment back to the viewer.

Across the page, below, is a sketch which shows the mechanics which an artist uses to find out how the fields and roads work in a composition. Yet even this tiny and simple sketch, not made to be a painting at all, has a very different feel. The winding road stretching directly ahead of the viewer seems almost a challenge – where will it go? – and although it has neither smoking chimney nor moving tractor, and was literally only a model for working, it is a much more active, much more experimental, more apprehensive, even, than the other two works.

Finally, there is a watercolour painting of a beach, its grey sky and grey stones making it unmistakably East Anglian. Here is quite a different approach; the landscape is left to speak for itself, with all the use of colour and atmospheric perspective, with the additional help of the roofs and jetties to stretch out the view far beyond the farmland or the road.

Because of this, at first glance it may say less about what I see than it says about the kind of countryside it is, the sort of people who live there, the quiet edge of a coastal village which must have been there for centuries. But in the end it is an image which I have imposed on the landscape, by selecting particular places and details, by choosing a wide-open foreground, a few lonely masts. Look long and hard at all your subjects, but remember that with landscapes, and especially with distant landscapes, you can achieve quite remarkable emotional links with the viewer by the simplest means.

Glossary

Abstract art. Art that does not try to represent recognizable objects, but uses form, colour and texture for their own aesthetic ends.

Abstract Expressionism. School of painting developed in New York in the 1940s, characterized by spontaneous expression through abstract forms. The most extreme type of Abstract Expressionism was Action painting, in which paint was splashed, thrown or dribbled over the canvas, Jackson Pollock was its most famous exponent.

Acrylic paint. Versatile, quick-drying synthetic paint, now a rival to oil paint in popularity. It is soluble in water, but can also be used with a special polymer medium.

Action painting. See Abstract Expressionism.

Aerial perspective. Effect caused by haze in the atmosphere whereby distant parts of a landscape appear bluish, their outlines blurred.

Alla prima. Technique in which the final surface of a picture is completed at one sitting, without underpainting. The term (Italian for 'at first') is used mostly of oil painting.

Aquatint. An etching process producing soft tonal gradations rather than firm lines.

Armory Show. Influential show of modern art held in New York in 1913. Its correct title is the International Exhibition of Modern Art; the popular name derives from the army building in which it was held.

Art Nouveau. Style that achieved popularity in all the visual arts from about 1890 to World War One. This 'new art' was characterized by flowing, plant-like forms.

Ashcan School. Group of late nineteenth-century and early twentieth-century American painters who depicted city life in a Realist way. They were most active in New York.

Barbizon School. Group of nineteenth-century French landscape painters who worked in and around the village of Barbizon in the forest of Fontainebleau. The naturalistic, uncontrived approach of the school presaged Impressionism.

Baroque. Term applied to the dominant style of European art from the early seventeenth to the early eighteenth century, characterized by panache and a sense of movement. Loosely, the term is sometimes used as a general label for the seventeenth century, as in the phrase 'the Age of Baroque'.

Bauhaus. School of design founded by the architect Gropius in Weimer in 1919, and later based in Dessau and Berlin until closed by the Nazis in 1933. The Bauhaus ideals of integrating art, craft and technology were enormously influential.

Bloom. Discoloured film that appears with age on varnished surfaces.

Body colour. Any paint that is opaque rather than transparent, but more particularly watercolour mixed with white. To all intents and purposes the term is a synonym for gouache.

Bole. Browny red clay sometimes used as a material for underpainting. It often shows through when the pigments on top of it fade or are abraded.

Cadmiums. Group of pigments made from cadmium sulphate and noted for their brilliance and permanence.

Calligraphy. Handwriting when considered as an art or craft.

Camden Town Group. Group of English painters active just before World War One, and living in the north London suburb of Camden Town. They are noted for works depicting unidealized urban scenes.

Camera Obscura. A room or a box in which an image of an outside scene can be projected by means of a lens onto a flat surface. It was sometimes used (for example by Canaletto) as an aid to accuracy in topographical painting.

Cartoon. A full-size drawing used to transfer a design to the painting surface, or to a tapestry. Today the word is more commonly used to mean a humorous drawing.

Charcoal. Sticks for drawing, processed from charred willow or vine-wood twigs.

Chiaroscuro. The effect of light and shade in a painting, a word derived from the Italian for 'bright-dark'. Usually it refers to paintings with strong tonal contrasts, most notably in the work of Caravaggio and his followers.

Chinese ink. See Indian ink.

Cinquecento. See Quattrocento.

Classicism. Term describing the ordered harmony and restraint associated with the art of classical Greece and Rome. The word is used in various ways and may, for example, refer to direct imitation of classical models, or, much more loosely, to art that is more concerned with preserving traditional values than with personal expression.

Cloisonnisme. Style of painting, first developed by Émile Bernard, in which strong flat areas of colour are outlined with dark contours, in the manner of *cloisonné* enamels.

Collage. A picture or design made by sticking pieces of paper or other essentially flat objects onto a flat surface. From the French '*coller*', to stick. See also *Papier collé*.

Colour field painting. Type of abstract painting characterized by broad expanses of unvariegated colour. Rothko was leading exponent.

Complementary colour. See Primary colours.

Conté. A type of hard crayon, named after its inventor, an eighteenty-century French scientist.

Copal. A resin derived from trees and used to make varnish and paint media.

Cubism. Style in painting and sculpture developed from 1907 by Picasso and Braque, and one of the most important turning points in European art. Cubist works broke down the forms of the objects they depicted into a multiplicity of facets, rather than showing them from a single viewpoint. The term Cubism was first applied derisively. The movement led the way to Abstract art.

Dada. Early twentieth-century international art movement, a forerunner of Surrealism. A product of the cynicism and bitterness engendered by World War One, the movement stressed irrationality and irreverence towards accepted standards. The world 'dada' (French for 'hobbyhorse') was chosen at random from a dictionary, reflecting this irrationality.

De Stijl. Dutch abstract art movement, at its height in the 1920s, that was inspired by ideas advocated in a magazine of the same name. The words are Dutch for 'the style'. The movement influenced the Bauhaus School. See also Neo-Plasticism.

Diptych. A work of art consisting of two linked (often hinged) panels or sections. A triptych has three panels, a polyptych four or more.

Distemper. A water-based paint used for large-scale paintings. It is not as permanent as fresco, and is used, for example, in theatrical scene-painting.

Donkey. Apparatus consisting of a low bench (astride which the artist sits) with a sloping board at one end to support a drawing or painting.

Dry brush. Technique in which a brush drags or skims undiluted paint over the surface of a painting so that the paint is left only on raised points, to create a broken effect.

Earth colour. Pigments derived from metal oxides, for example yellow ochre and terreverte.

Easel. A stand on which the artist supports the picture when painting. Sketching easels are light and collapsible; the largest studio easels are virtually items of furniture.

Encaustic. Technique of wall-painting by means of applying colours mixed with hot wax – the term derives from the Greek for 'to burn in'. It was popular in the ancient world and sporadic attempts have been made to revive it.

Engraving. General term applied to various techniques of creating a picture or design by incising lines on metal, wood or other materials. The term applies also to prints made by any of these processes.

Etching. An engraving technique in which the design is drawn in a thin layer of wax applied to a metal plate. The plate is immersed in acid, which eats away the metal only where the wax has been removed. When the wax has been melted off, the plate is inked and a print (also called an etching) can be made.

Expressionism. In its most general sense, a quality of emotional expressiveness in the arts gained through distortion and exaggeration. More specifically, the term is used in connection with north European, particularly German, painting in the early twentieth century.

Extender. Material added to paint to increase its bulk, known also as filler. It is generally used with cheaper quality paints.

Fat. Term applied to paint that is rich in oil 'Lean' refers to paint thinned with spirit such as turpentine.

Fauvism. Style practised by Matisse and a number of other French painters from 1905 to 1907. Their works, characterized by distorted shapes and very bright, unnaturalistic colours, outraged critics, one of whom dubbed them '*Les Fauves*' ('wild beasts').

Ferrule. The metal part of a brush that connects the bristles to the handle.

Figurative art. Art that represents recognizable objects, particularly the human figure, as distinct from Abstract art. Also known as Representational art.

Filbert. A brush whose bristles form a flat, tapering shape.

Fixative. Type of varnish sprayed onto drawings (particularly pastels) as a protective layer, to prevent their being smudged.

Foreshortening. The representation of an object so as to make it appear to project or recede. It may be thought of as perspective applied to an individual form.

Found object. Any object that an artist considers worthy of contemplation or exhibiting as a work of art without its being altered in any way. *Objet trouvé* is the French term.

Fresco. Technique of painting with water-based paints onto a wall covered with wet plaster. The pigment bonds chemically with the plaster, making the painting extremely durable. The term is often used incorrectly of any kind of mural painting. Leonardo da Vinci's famous *Last Supper*, for example, is often called a fresco, but in fact is the product of a complex experimental technique which partly accounts for its poor state of preservation.

Fugitive. Term applied to pigments that fade away especially when exposed to sunlight.

Futurism. Italian artistic and literary movement flourishing from 1909 to about 1915. It expressed the dynamism of the new machine age.

Genre. In its most general sense, a distinctive type of work of art. Thus landscapes and portraits are two genres of painting, just as plays and novels are genres of literature. In a more restricted sense, the term is applied to scenes of everyday life. The latter sense is the more common in discussions of painting.

Gesso. A mixture of gypsum and glue used as a priming on panels and canvases in the Middle Ages and Renaissance to provide a smooth, brilliant white surface.

Gilding. The application of gold leaf to a surface.

Glaze. A translucent layer of paint that modifies the colour of the paint underneath. In oil painting it can produce very subtle luminous effects, as in the work of Jan van Eyck.

Gouache. Opaque watercolour paint.

Graphite. A form of carbon, used in making the 'lead' of pencils.

Grisaille. A painting executed exclusively in one colour, especially grey, sienna, or a similar neutral colour, from '*gris*', the French for 'grey'.

Gum arabic. Sap exuded by certain acacia trees, used as a binding medium in water-based paints.

Half-tones. Rather vague term applied to the tones in a picture between the lightest and darkest tones.

Hatching. Technique of creating tonal effects in drawing or engraving by means of closely spaced parallel lines.

History painting. Painting representing themes from history, mythology, the Bible or great literature. In conventional academic theory up to the nineteenth century it was considered the most important and elevated branch of painting.

Hudson River School. Group of nineteenth-century American landscape painters who depicted the Hudson River Valley and other spectacular scenery.

Hue. The title of a colour, the attribute that distinguishes, say, blue from yellow.

Icon. An image of a saint or other religious personage, especially in the Byzantine, Greek Orthodox and Russian Orthodox Churches.

Illusionism. The use of various techniques in art to create the effect of real space or form on a two-dimensional surface. One type is *trompe l'oeil* (French for 'deceive the eye') in which, for instance, a fly may be painted on a picture-frame in minute, naturalistic detail so that the spectator takes it for a real insect.

Impasto. Paint applied very thickly, to create a textured surface.

Impressionism. Movement in nineteenth-century painting, originating in France in the 1860s. Characterized by a desire to show an image of what the eye sees at a particular moment, it was the most important artistic movement of the nineteenth century, many later movements being either developments from it or reactions to it.

Indian ink. A dense black ink available either as a liquid or in solid cakes.

Key. The prevailing tone of a painting. A predominantly light painting is said to have a high key, a predominantly dark one a low key.

Lean. See Fat.

Lightfast. Term applied to pigments that resist fading when exposed to sunlight, the opposite of Fugitive.

Limner. An archaic term for a painter, in particular a painter of miniatures. Nicholas Hilliard, the greatest of all Elizabethan miniaturists, wrote a treatise called *The Art of Limning*.

Local colour. The 'objective' colour of an object or surface, independent of any modifications caused by, for example, reflections or atmospheric conditions. Thus the local colour of a distant hillside may be green, even though to the eye it looks blue. See Aerial perspective.

Mannerism. The dominant style in European art from about 1520 to 1600. It was characterized by self-consciousness and hyper-sophistication marking a reaction against the serene classicism of the High Renaissance.

Mastic. Resin obtained from trees, used to make varnishes and paint media.

Medium. The word has two distinct meanings: (1) The substance with which pigment is mixed to make it flow in such a way that it can be applied with a brush. For example, water is the medium in watercolour, egg yolk in tempera. (2) In a more general sense the term refers to the material of which any work of art is created – oils or acrylics, for instance, or, with reference to a statue, bronze or marble.

Minimal art. Type of abstract art that, in reaction to the emotionalism of Abstract Expressionism, used only very basic geometric shapes and flat colours.

Modelling. The suggestion of the three-dimensionality of objects in drawing and painting by such means as hatching and tonal variations.

Monochrome. A painting or drawing executed in any one colour.

Montage. A picture created by combining several readymade images (such as photographs) or similar elements. The technique was used by the Cubists, and by many Pop artists.

Mural. A painting on a wall. See also Fresco.

Naïve painting. Painting done in a style that superficially looks childlike or untrained.

Naturalism. The representation of objects or scenes in an accurate, unidealized, objective way. The worlds 'naturalism' and 'realism' are often used interchangeably, but Realism (with a capital R) can refer also to a specific movement in nineteenth-century French painting, in which Courbet was the most important figure. Used in the latter sense, the term Realism implies a concern with low life or even squalid subjects, often with political overtones.

Neo-Classicism. The dominant style in European art in the late eighteenth and early nineteenth centuries. Characterized at its purest by severely classical forms and lofty moral ideas, the style marked a reaction against the frivolities of Rococo and was to some extent inspired by archaeological discoveries such as those at Pompeii.

Neo-Impressionism. A system of painting employing small touches of pure colour placed side by side so that they mix not on the canvas but in the viewer's eye. Neo-Impressionism, known also as Divisionism and Pointillism, was an offshoot of Impressionism and an attempt to make it more rational. Seurat was its main theorist and practitioner.

Neo-Plasticism. The name given by Mondrian to the style of abstract art that he and other members of De Stijl advocated and practised. It was a radically simple style, allowing little more than the primary colours and right-angled forms as means of expression.

Neue Sachlichkeit. German term meaning 'new objectivity' applied to a group of German painters active in the 1920s and 1930s whose works made strong social comments. Dix and Grosz were the two leading painters involved.

New Objectivity. See *Neue Sachlichkeit*.

Nocturne. A night scene. Whistler was the most celebrated practitioner and often used the word – originally a musical term – in the title of his paintings.

Novecento. See Quattrocento.

Objet trouvé. See Found Object.

Ochre. Name given to various pigments made from natural earth, also used generically for earth colours.

Oil paint. Paint in which the pigment is mixed with any of the various drying oils, the most common being linseed oil, which is made from flax. Oil paint is supremely versatile, allowing the creation of surfaces ranging from porcelain smoothness to violently expressive impasto; consequently it has been the dominant medium in European painting from the sixteenth century to the present day.

Op Art. Term applied to painting, especially that of the 1960s, that depended on dazzling optical effects to create visual illusions including, often, an impression of movement. Vasarély and the English painter Bridget Riley were leading exponents.

Ottocento. See Quattrocento.

Palette. The flat board, usually held in the hand by means of a thumb-hole, on which an artist lays out and mixes paint. The term can be applied also to the range of colours characteristic of a painter; thus Manet might be said to have a light palette and Caravaggio a sombre palette.

Papier collé. A picture created by cutting out pieces of paper and glueing them to a flat surface. It is a form of collage, and the technique was practised by the Cubists. The term is French for 'glued paper'. A similar technique is *découpage* (French for 'cutting out'), the decoration of a surface with paper cut-outs.

Pastel. Paint in the form of powdered colour bound with gum into sticks resembling wax crayons. Pastels are unique among paints in that they use no medium – the gum is simply there to hold the pigment together, and the paint is dry when applied (although it needs a fixative to hold it in place).

Perspective. Means of representing three-dimensional forms and spaces on a flat, i.e two-dimensional, surface.

Picture plane. The plane on which the imaginary space of a picture begins: in effect the surface of the picture. In certain Illusionist pictures, forms may appear to project from the picture plane as well as to recede behind it.

Picturesque. Aesthetic attitude, common in the eighteenth century, that took delight in irregularity and curiousness of forms, as, for example, in ruined buildings. Nowadays the meaning of the term has changed and it is generally applied to any view that is conventionally pleasing to look at.

Pigment. The colouring-matter of paint. The medium with which the pigment is mixed determines the qualities of the paint. Pigments are now usually synthesized chemically, but they were originally derived from a variety of animal, vegetable and mineral products.

Plastic. Term describing something that has been modelled or moulded. It can be used also to describe forms in paintings that seem to convey a particularly strong feeling of three-dimensionality.

Plein air. French term meaning 'open air', applied to pictures executed out of doors.

Pointillism. See Neo-Impressionism.

Polyptych. See Diptych.

Pop Art. Movement in art originating in the 1950s and taking as its subject-matter products of the contemporary consumer society and mass media. Andy Warhol's famous paintings of soup-cans are among the most characteristic images of the movement.

Poster paint. A fairly inexpensive form of opaque water-colour used mainly for design work rather than paintings.

Post-Impressionism. General term applied to various trends in European painting in the period from about 1880 to about 1905. The term was first used in 1910 by the English art critic and painter Roger Fry as the title of an exhibition dominated by the work of Cézanne, Gauguin and van Gogh, the three giants of Post-Impressionism.

Post-Painterly Abstraction. Term applied to various styles of painting developed in America in the 1950s and 1960s. Reacting against the extreme subjectivity of Abstract Expressionism, the Post-Painterly Abstractionists created much more dispassionate paintings, often characterized by hard-edged areas of flat colour.

Pre-Raphaelite Brotherhoold ('PRB'). Group of young British painters formed in 1848 with the aim of reviving what they considered the high moral tone of painting before Raphael. Although short-lived, the group was very influential. Millais and Rossetti were among the founder-members.

Primary colours. In painting, the colours that cannot be created by mixing other colours – that is, blue, red and yellow. Secondary colours are those created by mixing two primary colours; thus blue and yellow create green. A complementary colour is one having the maximum contrast with another colour; thus orange (a mixture of red and yellow) is the complementary of blue.

Priming. A layer or layers of material applied to a canvas, panel or other painting support to make it more suitable to receive paint by, for example, rendering it smoother or less absorbent. Gesso is historically the best-known priming material.

Quattrocento. Italian term, meaning literally 'four hundred', used as a period label for the fifteenth century (the 1400s). It can be used as an adjective as well as a noun, as in the expression 'a Quattrocento painting'. Corresponding Italian terms are used in a similar way: Trecento for the fourteenth century, Cinquecento for the sixteenth century, Seicento for the seventeenth century, Settecento for the eighteenth century, Ottocento for the nineteenth century, and Novocento for the twentieth century.

Realism. See Naturalism.

Renaissance. Term (French for 'rebirth') applied to an intellectual and artistic movement originating in Italy and founded on a revival and re-interpretation of classical culture. The chronological boundaries of the Renaissance are ill-defined, its origins in art being sometimes placed as early as Giotto. The brief period in the first two decades of the sixteenth century, when the movement reached a peak of balance and harmony in the work of artists such as Raphael, is known as the High Renaissance. The Renaissance gradually spread throughout Europe, and the term Northern Renaissance is applied to its dissemination outside Italy.

Representational art. Another term for Figurative art.

Rococo. Frothy, elegant style developed out of Baroque at the beginning of the eighteenth century. Boucher is a quintessentially Rococo artist.

Romanticism. Intellectual and artistic movement flourishing from about 1780 to about 1840. In contrast to the contemporary Neo-Classical style, Romanticism involved the subjective expression of emotion, often through dynamic forms and vibrant colours.

Salon des Refusés. Exhibition held in 1863 to show paintings, among them Manet's *Olympia*, rejected by the official Salon. It is regarded as a momentous event in the development of modern art.

Sanguine. Red chalk, one of the most common drawing materials.

Scumble. Opaque paint dragged over another layer of paint so that the underlying colour shows through in parts.

Secondary colour. See Primary colour.

Seicento. See Quattrocento.

Settecento. See Quattrocento.

Sfumato. Tones blended with imperceptibly

subtle transitions (the word is Italian for 'evaporated'). Leonardo da Vinci was the most famous exponent of the technique.

Silverpoint. Drawing technique using a silver-tipped instrument and specially prepared paper. It was popular during the Renaissance and could produce exquisitely delicate effects, but later fell into disuse, probably because the lines cannot easily be erased.

Size. A form of glue used to prime canvases or panels.

Social Realism. Realist painting in which the subject has overtly social or political content. It is not to be confused with Socialist Realism, which is a name given to the official (and usually very dull) art promoted by the state in countries such as the Soviet Union.

Stippling. Technique of shading in drawing and painting, using closely spaced dots rather than lines.

Support. The surface to which paint is applied. Canvas, wooden panels and walls (in mural painting) are all supports. Most supports need to be coated with priming before they can be painted on.

Surrealism. Literary and artistic movement of the 1920s and 1930s. It was characterized by the use of bizarre, incongruous and irrational elements.

Tempera. Paint using eggs as the medium. It was overtaken in popularity by oil paint during the Renaissance.

Tenebrism. A quality of overall darkness of tone in a painting. Derived from an Italian word for 'obscure' ('*tenebroso*'), the term is associated particularly with Caravaggio and his followers.

Tone. Term describing the degree of darkness or lightness of a colour.

Tooth. The degree of roughness of a canvas or other support.

Tecento. See Quattrocento.

Triptych. See Diptych.

Trompe l'oeil. See Illusionism.

Ultramarine. See Pigment.

Value. The lightness or darkness of a colour, essentially a synonym for tone, although the term is sometimes used in rather unclear ways.

Vanishing point. A point on the horizon at which receding parallel lines appear to meet, a term commonly used in connection with perspective.

Wash. A thin, usually broadly applied, layer of transparent pigment such as watercolour or ink.

Watercolour. Pigment bound with gum arabic and diluted with water in use. Watercolour is traditionally used to create translucent effects, white highlights being produced by leaving the paper blank.

Museums and Galleries

United Kingdom

The following is a selective list of United Kingdom art galleries and museums, arranged alphabetically by country.

ENGLAND

Avon

Bristol City Art Gallery, Queen's Road, Clifton, Bristol. (Bristol 299771) International collection up till present day.

David Cross Fine Art Gallery, 3a Boyce's Avenue, Clifton, Bristol. (Bristol 732614) Marine art, Bristol School.

Royal West of England Academy, Queen's Road, Clifton, Bristol. (Bristol 735129) 20th-century paintings.

Victoria Art Gallery, Bridge Street, Bath. (Bath 61111) Old masters; paintings of 18th to 20th century.

Bedfordshire

Cecil Higgins Art Gallery, Castle Close, Bedford. (Bedford 211222) English watercolours.

Luton Museum and Art Gallery, Wardown Park, Luton. (Luton 36941) Topographical watercolours, oils.

Berkshire

Reading Museum and Art Gallery, Blagrave Street, Reading. (Reading 55911) 19th- and 20th-century British paintings.

Buckinghamshire

David Messum Fine Paintings Ltd, 22a and 26 London End, Beaconsfield. (Beaconsfield 77578) 18th-, 19th-century British oils; French and English watercolours; contemporary art.

Cambridgeshire

Cambridge Fine Art Ltd, 68 Trumpington Street, Cambridge. (Cambridge 68488) Victorian oils and watercolours.

Fitzwilliam Museum, Trumpington Street, Cambridge. (Cambridge 69501) Very wide international collection includes Titian, Veronese, Hogarth, Impressionists.

Kettle's Yard, Northampton Street, Cambridge. (Cambridge 352124) 20th-century art.

Peterborough City Museum and Art Gallery, Priestgate, Peterborough. (Peterborough 43329) Changing exhibitions of contemporary art; local portraits and topographical works.

Cheshire

Warrington Museum and Art Gallery, Bold Street, Warrington. (Warrington 30550) 18th- and 19th-century paintings.

Cleveland

Billingham Art Gallery, Queen's Way, Billingham. (Middlesbrough 555443) 20th-century oils, watercolours.

Gray Art Gallery and Museum, Clarence Road, Hartlepool. (Hartlepool 68916) 19th- and 20th-century oils and watercolours; marine paintings; local artists.

Middlesbrough Art Gallery, 320 Linthorpe Road, Middlesbrough. (Middlesbrough 247445) Old masters; 20th-century British art.

Cornwall

Falmouth Art Gallery, The Moor, Falmouth. (Falmouth 313863) Late 19th- and 20th-century British works.

Newlyn Orion Galleries, New Road, Newlyn, Penzance. (Penzance 3715) Contemporary painting.

Royal Institution of Cornwall, Art Gallery, River Street, Truro. (Truro 2205) 18th- and 19th-century drawings.

Cumbria

Abbot Hall Art Gallery, Abbot Hall, Kendal. (Kendal 22464) Leading 20th-century artists including Nicholson, Piper; 18th-century portraits; 18th- and 19th-century watercolours.

Carlisle Museum and Art Gallery, Castle Street, Carlisle. (Carlisle 34781) 19th- and 20th-century works.

Fitz Park Museum and Art Gallery, Station Road, Keswick. (Keswick 73263) Works by Turner, Steer; local artists.

Derbyshire

Derby Museums and Art Gallery, The Strand, Derby. (Derby 31111) Scientific and other paintings by Joseph Wright; local topographical works.

Devon

Burton Art Gallery, Victoria Park, Kingsley Road, Bideford. (Bideford 6711) Late 19th- and 20th-century British art.

Plymouth City Museum and Art Gallery, Drake Circus, Plymouth. (Plymouth 668000) Old master drawings; 18th- and 19th-century English works; Camden Town Group.

Royal Albert Memorial Museum and Art Gallery, Queen Street, Exeter. (Exeter 56724) 18th- and 19th-century English oils, watercolours; Devon artists.

Devon

Hambledon Gallery, 42 Salisbury Street, Blandford. (Blandford 52880) Contemporary works by British artists.

Melbury Gallery, 21 High Street, Shaftesbury. (Shaftesbury 4428) Contemporary art, especially by leading artists.

Red House Museum and Art Gallery, Quay Road, Christchurch. (Christchurch 482860) Monthly exhibitions of mostly 20th-century British art.

Russell Cotes Art Gallery and Museum, East Cliff, Bournemouth. (Bournemouth 21009) 17th- to 20th-century art.

The Studio, King's Arms Yard, High Street, Dorchester. (Dorchester 66828) 19th- and 20th-century paintings, mainly British.

Durham

Darlington Art Gallery, Crown Street, Darlington. (Darlington 62034) 19th- and 20th-century oils and watercolours, including Brangwyn, Sutherland; regional professional artists.

Essex

Beecroft Art Gallery, Station Road, Westcliff-on-Sea. (Southend-on-Sea 347418) British and continental old masters; 20th-century artists; local topographical works.

The Minories, 74 High Street, Colchester. (Colchester 77067) Contemporary and historical works; Constable drawings.

Playhouse Gallery, The High, Harlow. (Harlow 33351) Mostly contemporary British artists.

Gloucestershire

Cheltenham Art Gallery and Museum, 40 Clarence Street, Cheltenham. (Cheltenham 37431) 17th-century Dutch paintings; 19th- and 20th-century British works.

City Museum and Art Gallery, Brunswick Road, Gloucester. (Gloucester 24131) Italian primitives; Breughel; 18th- and 19th-century English artists, including Gainsborough; 20th-century works.

Henry-Brett Gallery, Holford House, Bourton-on-the-Water. (Bourton-on-the-Water 20443) Landscapes, wild life and sporting art.

Greater Manchester

Astley-Cheetham Art Gallery, Trinity Street, Stalybridge. (061-338 3831) Late-medieval to Renaissance; 18th- and 19th-century paintings.

Bury Art Gallery and Museum, Moss Street, Bury. (061-761 4021) Mainly 19th-century British works, including Constable, Turner, Landseer.

City Art Gallery, Mosley Street, Manchester. (061-236 9422) Old masters, Gainsborough, Turner, Pre-Raphaelites.

Gallery of Modern Art, Princess Street, Manchester. (061-236 9422) 20th-century British art.

Henry Donn Gallery, 138–142 Bury New Road, Whitefield, Manchester. (061-766 8819) Mostly 20th-century British art.

Tib Lane Gallery, 14a Tib Lane, Manchester. (061-834 6928) Mainly figurative British, 20th-century paintings, drawings.

Whitworth Art Gallery, Whitworth Park, Manchester. (061-273 4865) Large permanent collection from all periods: Blake, Pre-Raphaelites, Cézanne, van Gogh, Hockney.

Hampshire

Portsmouth City Museum and Art Gallery, Museum Road, Old Portsmouth. (Portsmouth 827261) 17th- to 20th-century and local topographical paintings and drawings.

St Peter's Gallery, Chesil Street, Winchester. (Winchester 68901) 18th- to 20th-century English paintings.

Southampton Art Gallery, Civic Centre, Southampton. (Southampton 23855) Large, wide-ranging collection including van Dyck, Renoir; contemporary works.

Winchester School of Art Exhibitions Gallery, Park Avenue, Winchester. (Winchester 61891) Mostly contemporary art.

Hereford and Worcester
Kidderminster Art Gallery, Market Street, Kidderminster. (Kidderminster 66610) 18th- to 20th-century works.

Lower Nupend Gallery, Cradley, near Malvern. (Ridgway Cross 334) English arts, 18th to early 20th-century.

Worcester City Art Gallery, Foregate Street, Worcester. (Worcester 25371) Early English watercolours; Victorian oils; contemporary works.

Hertfordshire
Hitchin Museum and Art Gallery, Paynes Park, Hitchin. (Hitchin 4476) Local 19th- and 20th-century watercolours.

Humberside
Beverley Art Gallery, Champney Road, Beverley. (Hull 882255) Local artists; permanent collection.

Ferens Art Gallery, Queen Victoria Square, Hull. (Hull 222750) Old masters, English 18th- and 19th-century portraits, local marine paintings, contemporary works.

Kent
Nevill Gallery, 43 St Peter's Street, Canterbury. (Canterbury 65291) Period and contemporary oils and watercolours.

New Metropole Arts Centre, The Leas, Folkestone. (Folkestone 55070) Contemporary and historical exhibitions.

Lancashire
Blackburn Museum and Art Gallery, Library Street, Blackburn. (Blackburn 667130) Victorian oils, including Leighton.

Bolton Museum and Art Gallery, Le Mans Crescent, Bolton. (Bolton 22311) 17th- to 20th-century works, mostly British.

Grundy Art Gallery, Queen Street, Blackpool. (Blackpool 23977) 19th- and 20th-century works, including John Nash.

Harris Museum and Art Gallery, Market Square, Preston. (Preston 58248) 19th- and early 20th-century British art.

Leicestershire
Leicestershire Museum and Art Gallery, 97 New Walk, Leicester. (Leicester 554100) 17th- to 20th-century British art; French Impressionists; German Expressionists.

Lincolnshire
Usher Gallery, Lindum Road, Lincoln. (Lincoln 27980) Contemporary art; European historical art.

London
Bankside Gallery, 48 Hopton Street, SE1. (01-928 7521) Exhibitions by, among others, members of Royal Society of Painters in Watercolours.

Blackheath Gallery, 34a Tranquil Vale, SE3. (01-852 1802) Contemporary oils, watercolours; Victorian watercolours.

Camden Arts Centre, Arkwright Road, NW3. (01-435 2643) Contemporary art.

Courtauld Institute Galleries, Woburn Square, WC1. (01-580 1015) Old masters, French Impressionists, Post-Impressionists, Roger Fry Collection, English watercolours.

Dulwich Picture Gallery, College Road, SE21. (01-693 5254) Old masters, including Rembrandt, Rubens, Claude, Poussin, Reynolds, Gainsborough, van Dyck, Raphael.

Hayward Gallery, Southbank, SE1. (01-928 3144) Wide variety of exhibitions by the Arts Council of Great Britain.

Institute of Contemporary Arts, Nash House, The Mall, SW1. (01-930 0493) New developments in art.

Kenwood House, Hampstead Lane, NW3. (01-348 1286) Rembrandt, Vermeer, Gainsborough, Reynolds.

Leighton House, 12 Holland Park Road, W14. (01-602 3316) High Victorian art, including works by Burne-Jones etc.

Mall Galleries, The Mall, SW1. (01-930 6844) Annual exhibitions of major national Art Societies.

National Gallery, Trafalgar Square, WC2. (01-839 3321) Western European art from 14th to 20th century, a vast collection that includes Leonardo, Titian, Turner, Picasso.

National Portrait Gallery, 2 St Martin's Place, WC2. (01-930 1552) British portraits, medieval times to present day.

Queen's Gallery, Buckingham Palace Road, SW1. (01-930 4832) Works from the Royal Collection.

Royal Academy of Arts, Burlington House, Piccadilly, W1. (01-734 9052) Old master collection; annual Summer Exhibitions and other temporary exhibitions.

Serpentine Gallery, Kensington Gardens, W2. (01-402 6075) Contemporary works in all media.

South London Art Gallery, Peckham Road, SE5. (01-703 6120) British paintings from 18th century to present day.

Tate Gallery, Millbank, SW1. (01-821 1313) Major collection of British paintings of all periods; modern foreign patterns.

Victoria and Albert Museum, Cromwell Road, South Kensington, SW7. (01-589 6371) International collection of all periods; Raphael cartoons, Constable paintings.

Wallace Collection, Hertford House, Manchester Square, W1. (01-935 0687) Fine old master collection, including Poussin, Boucher, Murillo, Velazquez. Hals.

Whitechapel Gallery, 80 Whitechapel High Street, E1. (01-377 0107) Temporary exhibitions of contemporary art.

William Morris Gallery, Water House, Lloyd Park, Forest Road, Walthamstow, E17. (01-527 5544) Victorian art.

Merseyside
Atkinson Art Gallery, Lord Street, Southport. (Southport 33133) 18th- to 20th-century British oils, watercolours.

Lady Lever Art Gallery, Port Sunlight Village, Wirral. (051-645 3623) Mainly British artists, including Pre-Raphaelites.

St Helens Museum and Art Gallery, College Street, St Helens. (St Helens 24061) Contemporary and historical.

Walker Art Gallery, William Brown Street, Liverpool. (051-227 5234) 14th- to 16th-century Italian, Netherlandish and German paintings; 17th- to 20th-century English paintings; 17th-century old masters; 19th-century French paintings.

Williamson Art Gallery and Museum, Slatey Road, Birkenhead. (051-652 4177) Contemporary and historical; 18th- to 20th-century English watercolours; Liverpoool School.

Norfolk
Castle Museum, Norwich. (Norwich 611277) Dutch and English paintings, including Norwich School.

Sainsbury Centre for Visual Arts, University of East Anglia, Norwich. (Norwich 56161) Mostly contemporary art.

Northamptonshire
Central Museum and Art Gallery, Guildhall Road, Northampton. (Northampton 34881) 17th- and 18th-century Italian paintings; English watercolours; local contemporary artists.

Northumberland
Stocksfield Studio Gallery, Branch End, Stocksfield. (Stocksfield 3065) Specializes in north-of-England landscapes.

Nottinghamshire
Castle Museum and Art Gallery, Castle Gate, Nottingham. (Nottingham 411881) 17th-century Dutch paintings; 18th-century English School; Bonington; Victorian paintings; 20th-century works, including Lowry.

Mansfield Museum and Art Gallery, Leeming Street, Mansfield. (Mansfield 22561) Local watercolours.

Nottingham University Art Gallery, Portland Building, University Park, Nottingham. (Nottingham 56101) Changing exhibitions, from old masters to contemporary art.

Oxfordshire
Ashmolean Museum, Beaumont Street, Oxford. (Oxford 512651) Wide-ranging collection of European art includes 16th- and 17th-century Italian paintings; Dutch and Flemish still lifes; French Impressionists (Pissarro); English School; drawings by Raphael, Michelangelo.

Christ Church Picture Gallery, Canterbury Quadrangle, Christ Church, Oxford. (Oxford

242102) Old master paintings (Tintoretto, Veronese, Hals, van Dyck) and drawings (Leonardo, Michelangelo, Raphael).

Museum of Modern Art, 30 Pembroke Street, Oxford. (Oxford 722733) 20th-century art.

Staffordshire
England's Gallery, 56–58 St Edward Street, Leek. (Leek 373451) From 17th century to contemporary art.

Hobbergate Art Gallery, Brampton Park, Newcastle under Lyme. (Newcastle under Lyme 611962) 18th- and 19th-century oils and watercolours by mostly local artists.

Stafford Museum and Art Gallery, The Green, Stafford. (Stafford 57303) Contemporary works, especially by local artists.

Stoke-on-Trent City Museum and Art Gallery, Broad Street, Hanley, Stoke-on-Trent. (Stoke-on-Trent 29611) Mainly British 18th- to 20th-century paintings, drawings, watercolours.

Suffolk
Bury St Edmunds Art Gallery, Market Cross, Bury St Edmunds. (Bury St Edmunds 62081) Wide variety of temporary exhibitions.

Gainsborough's House, Gainsborough Street, Sudbury. (Sudbury 72958) Gainsborough and other Suffolk artists.

Wolsey Art Gallery, Christchurch Mansion, Christchurch Park, Ipswich. (Ipswich 53246) Paintings by Suffolk artists, including Constable, Gainsborough; contemporary works.

Surrey
Bourne Gallery, 31–33 Lesbourne Road, Reigate. (Reigate 41614) 19th- and 20th-century English watercolours and oils

Michael Stewart Fine Art Galleries, 61 Quarry Street, Guildford. (Guildford 504359) Contemporary British artists; wildlife and sporting works.

Reid Gallery Ltd, Milkhouse Gate, High Street, Guildford. (Guildford 68912) Mainly British 19th- and 20th-century watercolours; contemporary oils and watercolours.

Sussex, East
Royal Pavilion Art Gallery and Museum, Church Street, Brighton. (Brighton 603005) Regency period British paintings; late 18th- and early 19th-century watercolours.

Hastings Museum and Art Gallery, John's Place, Cambridge Road, Hastings. (Hastings 435952) 18th- and 19th-century oils, watercolours and drawings of local interest.

Hove Museum of Art, 19 New Church Road, Hove. (Brighton 779410) 18th- to 20th-century works by mainly British artists, including Munnings, Orpen, Stanley Spencer.

Rye Art Gallery, East Street, Rye. (Rye 223218) British 20th-century artists, including Sutherland, Nash, Burra, Piper, Adrizzoni.

Towner Art Gallery, Manor Gardens, Borough Lane, Old Town, Eastbourne. (Eastbourne 21635) 19th- and 20th-century British art; wide variety of temporary exhibitions.

Sussex, West
Chichester House Gallery, High Street, Ditchling, Hassocks (Hassocks 4167) 18th- and 19th-century English watercolours and oil paintings.

Worthing Museum and Art Gallery, Chapel Road, Worthing. (Worthing 39999) Watercolours and oils from late 18th to mid-20th century; Pre-Raphaelites.

Tyne and Wear
Hatton Gallery, The University, Newcastle upon Tyne. (Newcastle upon Tyne 328511) 16th- to 18th-century European paintings; contemporary English paintings and drawings.

Laing Art Gallery, Higham Place, Newcastle upon Tyne. (Newcastle upon Tyne 326989) British oils and watercolours from 18th century to present day (Turner, Girtin, Palmer, Hockney).

Sunderland Museum and Art Gallery, Borough Road, Sunderland. (Sunderland 41235) 18th- to 20th-century works, especially by local artists (including Lowry).

Warwickshire
Kathleen Morris, Six Bells, Pathlow, Stratford-upon-Avon. (Stratford-upon-Avon 204350) Pre-Raphaelites and West Midlands artists.

Warwick District Council Art Gallery and Museum, Avenue Road, Leamington Spa. (Leamington Spa 26559) 20th-century oils and watercolours, mainly English; 16th-century Dutch and Flemish masters.

West Midlands
Birmingham City Museum and Art Gallery, Chamberlain Square, Birmingham. (021-235 2834) Major collection of Pre-Raphaelites; old masters; 17th-century Italian paintings; English watercolours.

Wolverhampton Art Gallery, Lichfield Street, Wolverhampton. (Wolverhampton 24549) 18th- to 20th-century English art – Gainsborough, Zoffany, Romney; Wyndham Lewis, Warhol, Peter Blake.

Wiltshire
Swindon Museum and Art Gallery, Bath Road, Swindon. (Swindon 26161) 20th-century British collection (not always on display) includes Lowry, Nash, Steer, Nicholson.

Yorkshire, North
York City Art Gallery, Exhibition Square, York. (York 23839) British and European paintings, including the Lycett Green collection of old masters (early Italian panel paintings); English School includes Reynolds, Etty.

Yorkshire, South
Doncaster Museum and Art Gallery, Chequer Road, Doncaster. (Doncaster 62095) European contemporary and historical works (Tiepolo, Lowry)

Graves Art Gallery, Surrey Street, Sheffield. (Sheffield 734781) 16th- to 20th-century British art, including Camden Town Group; European old masters.

Mappin Art Gallery, Weston Park, Sheffield. (Sheffield 26281) 18th- to 20th-century British art, with large Victorian collection; contemporary art with local links.

Yorkshire, West
Bradford Art Galleries and Museums, Cartwright Hall, Lister Park, Bradford. (Bradford 493313) Contemporary and historical European works.

Huddersfield Art Gallery, Princess Alexandra Walk, Huddersfield. (Huddersfield 21356) 19th-century to contemporary paintings and drawings (Camden Town Group).

Leeds City Art Gallery, The Headrow, Leeds. (Leeds 462495) Large collection includes Victorian oils, English watercolours (Cotman), 20th-century works.

Temple Newsam House, off A63 road, Leeds. (Leeds 647321) Country house collection of Italian, Dutch and English masters, including Guardi, Tiepolo, van Ruisdael, Stubbs; family portraits.

NORTHERN IRELAND
Ulster Museum, Botanic Gardens, Belfast. (Belfast 668251) Irish art from 17th century to present day; old masters; 18th- and 19th-century watercolours; international contemporary works.

SCOTLAND
Borders
Hawick Museum and Art Gallery, Wilton Lodge, Hawick. (Hawick 73457) Local topographical paintings.

Central
Stirling-Smith Art Gallery and Museum, 40 Albert Place, Dumbarton Road, Stirling. (Stirling 71917) Mostly British 19th-century oils and watercolours.

Dumfries and Galloway
Gracefield Arts Centre, 28 Edinburgh Road, Dumfries. (Dumfries 52301) Mostly Scottish 19th- and 20th-century oils, watercolours.

Fife
Kircaldy Museum and Art Gallery, War Memorial Gardens, Kircaldy. (Kircaldy 260732) Mainly 19th- and 20th-century Scottish; Camden Town Group; late 19th-century French paintings; contemporary works.

Grampian
Aberdeen Art Gallery and Museums, Schoolhill, Aberdeen. (Aberdeen 646333) 18th- to 20th-century art, including Impressionists and Post-Impressionists; contemporary painting.

Highland
Inverness Museum and Art Gallery, Castle Wynd, Inverness. (Inverness 237114) Art related to the Highlands, from 17th to 20th-century; temporary exhibitions.

Lothian
Bourne Fine Art, 4 Dundas Street, Edinburgh. (031-557 4050) 19th- and early 20th-century paintings; Glasgow School. Fine Art Scoeity, 12 Great King Street, Edinburgh. (031-556 0305) 19th- and 20th-century British art, with Scottish emphasis.

National Gallery of Scotland, The Mound, Edinburgh. (031-556 8921) Major collection of European painting up to 1900 – including

Titian, Raphael, Rembrandt, Constable, Turner, Impressionists; also, collection of drawings.

Royal Scottish Academy, The Mound, Edinburgh. (031-225 6671) International exhibitions and annual RSA exhibition; RSA Diploma collection.

Scottish National Gallery of Modern Art, Inverleith House, Royal Botanic Gardens, Edinburgh. (031-332 3754) 20th-century art, including Braque, Picasso, Moore, Hockney. (Gallery moves to 75 Belford Road, Edinburgh, in 1984).

Scottish National Portrait Gallery, 1 Queen Street, Edinburgh. (031-556 8921) Scottish portraits in all media, from 16th century to present day.

Strathclyde

Glasgow Art Gallery, Argyll Street, Kelvingrove, Glasgow. (041-334 1134) Major international works, including Impressionist collection.

Hunterian Art Gallery, University of Glasgow, Hillhead Street, Glasgow. (041-339 8855) International collection includes works by Rembrandt, Stubbs, Pissarro, Whistler, and Scottish artists from 18th century to present.

McLean Museum and Art Gallery, 9 Union Street, Greenock. (Greenock 23741) Mainly 19th-century Scottish School; other artists represented include Raeburn, Corot, Boudin.

Paisley Museum and Art Galleries, High Street, Paisley. (041-889 3151) Permanent collection includes Barbizon School and Camden Town Group (Sickert); contemporary Scottish art.

Tayside

Dundee Central Museum and Art Gallery, Albert Square, Dundee. (Dundee 27643) Historical and contemporary, with emphasis on Scottish painting; minor European old masters.

Perth Museum and Art Gallery, 78 George Street, Perth. (Perth 32488) 19th-century painting (including Millais, Landseer); Scottish artists.

WALES

Glamorgan, South

National Museum of Wales, Cathays Park, Cardiff. (Cardiff 397951) Art from the Renaissance to present day, including old masters, Rubens cartoons and 19th-century French Realists and Impressionists.

Gwent

Newport Museum and Art Gallery, John Frost Square, Newport. (Newport 840064) Early English watercolours; 20th-century British oils, with emphasis on Welsh artists.

International Galleries

ARGENTINA
Buenos Aires: Museo de Arte Moderno; Museo Nacional de Bellas Artes

AUSTRALIA
Adelaide: Art Gallery of South Australia
Brisbane: Queensland Art Gallery
Melbourne: National Gallery of Victoria
Perth: Art Gallery of Western Australia
Sydney: Art Gallery of New South Wales

AUSTRIA
Salzburg: Residenz Galerie
Vienna: Gemäldegaleri der Akademie der Bildenden Kunste; Kunsthistorisches Museum; Museum Moderner Kunst

BELGIUM
Antwerp: Koninklijk Museum voor Schone Kunsten
Brussels: Musées Royaux des Beaux-Arts de Belge
Liège: Musée d'Art Moderne

BRAZIL
Rio de Janeiro: Museu Nacional de Belas Arts
Sao Paolo: Museu de Arte; Museu de Arte Contemporanea

CANADA
Montreal: Musée des Beaux-Arts
Ottawa: National Gallery of Canada
Toronto: Art Gallery of Ontario
Vancouver: Vancouver Art Gallery

CZECHOSLOVAKIA
Prague: Narodni Galerie

DENMARK
Copenhagen: Statens Museum for Kunst

EAST GERMANY
Berlin: Nationalgalerie
Dresien: Barockmuseum; Staatliche Kunstsammlungen

EGYPT
Cairo: Museum of Islamic Art

FRANCE
Antibes: Musée Picasso
Aix-en-Provence: Musée Granet
Besançon: Musée des Beaux-Arts
Lyons: Musée des Beaux-Arts
Montpellier: Musée Fabre
Nice: Musée Matisse
Orléans: Musée des Beaux-Arts
Paris: Musée d'Art Moderne; Musée de l'Orangerie; Musée des Arts Decoratifs; Musée du Petit Palais; Musée du Louvre
Tours: Musée des Beaux-Arts

GREECE
Athens: Benaki Museum

HUNGARY
Budapest: Hungarian National Gallery; Museum of Fine Arts

POLAND
Litomerice: North Bohemian Gallery of Fine Arts
Poznan: National Museum
Warsaw: National Museum

PORTUGAL
Lisbon: Museu Calouste Gulbenkian

SOUTH AFRICA
Cape Town: Michaelis Collection; South African National Gallery
Durban: Museum and Art Gallery
Johannesburg: Africana Museum; Municipal Art Gallery
Port Elizabeth: King George VI Art Gallery

SPAIN
Barcelona: Museo de Arte de Cataluñs; Museo Picasso

INDIA
New Delhi: National Museum of India; Rabindra Bhavan Art Gallery
Trivandrum: Sri Chitra Art Gallery and Gallery of Asian Paintings

IRELAND
Dublin: Hugh Lane Municipal Gallery of Modern Art; National Gallery of Ireland

ISRAEL
Haifa: Museum of Modern Art
Tel Aviv: Tel Aviv Museum

ITALY
Bologna: Pinacoteca Nazionale
Florence: Galleria degli Uffizi; Galleria dell'Accademia; Palazzo Pitti
Milan: Galleria d'Arte Moderna; Museo d'Arte Antica; Pinacoteca Ambrosiana; Pinacoteca di Brera
Modena: Galleria, Museo e Medaglier Estense
Parma: Galleria Borghese; Galleria Nazionale d'Arte Moderna; Galleria Nazionale di Roma; Vatican Museums
Turin: Galleria Sabauda
Venice: Galleria dell'Accademia; Palazzo Ducale: Peggy Guggenheim Collection

JAPAN
Kurashiki: Ohara Art Gallery
Kyoto: Municipal Museum of Art; National Museum
Tokyo: National Museum; National Museum of Western Arts

MEXICO
Mexico City: Museo de Arte Moderno; Museo de San Carlos

NETHERLANDS
Amsterdam: Rembrandt-Huis Museum; Rijksmuseum; Rijksmuseum Vincent van Gogh
Groningen: Groningen Museum
Haarlem: Frans Halsmuseum
Rotterdam: Museum Boymans van Beuningen
The Hague: Gemeentemuseum; Mauritshuis

NEW ZEALAND
Auckland: City Art Gallery
Wanganui: Sarjeant Gallery
Wellington: National Art Gallery

NORWAY
Oslo: Munch-museet; Nasjonalgalleriet

PERU
Lima: Museo de Arte

Bilbao: Museo de Bellas Artes
Madrid: Museo del Prado; Museo Lázaro Galdiano

SWITZERLAND
Basil: Kunstmuseum Basel
Bern: Kunstmuseum
Geneva: Musée d'Art et d'Histoire
Winterthur: Kunstmuseum
Zurich: Kunsthaus

TURKEY
Istanbul: Topkapi Palace Museum

USA
Baltimore: Museum of Art; Walters Art Gallery
Boston: Museum of Fine Arts
Cambridge, Mass.: William Hayes Fogg Art Museum
Chicago: Art Institute
Cincinnati: Art Museum
Detroit: Institute of Arts
Houston: Museum of Fine Arts
Los Angeles: County Museum of Art; Huntingdon Art Gallery; J. Paul Getty Museum; Norton Simon Museum of Art
Manchester, N.H.: Currier Gallery of Art
Minneapolis: Society of Fine Arts
New Orleans: Museum of Art
New York: Frick Collection; Metropolitan Museum of Art; Museum of Modern Art; Solomon R. Guggenheim Museum; Whitney Museum of American Art
Philadelphia: Museum of Art
Richmond, V.A.: Virgina Museum of Fine Art
San Diego: Museum of Art
San Francisco: M.H. de Young Memorial Museum; Museum of Modern Art
Washington, D.C.: Freer Gallery of Art; National Gallery of Art; National Museum of American Art

USSR
Kiev: State Museum of Ukrainian Art; State Museum of Western and Oriental Art
Leningrad: State Hermitage Museum; State Russian Museum
Moscow: Kremlin Museum; State Pushkin Museum of Fine Arts; State Tretyakov Gallery

WEST GERMANY
Berlin: Nationalgalerie
Bonn: Rheinisches Landesmuseum; Städtisches Kunstmuseum
Munich: Alte Pinakothek; Neue Pinakothek; Staatsgalerie Moderner Kunst
Nuremburg: Albrecht Dürer Haus

YUGOSLAVIA
Ljubljana: Narodna Galerija

ZAMBIA
Livingstone: Livingstone Museum

ZIMBABWE
Harare: National Gallery of Zimbabwe

Index